Educating for
GLOBAL
COMPETENCE
2ND EDITION

Educating for GLOBAL

COMPETENCE

Preparing Our Students to Engage the World

· · · 2ND EDITION · · ·

VERONICA BOIX MANSILLA
Project Zero, Harvard Graduate
School of Education

ANTHONY W. JACKSON
Center for Global Education,
Asia Society

ascd

Arlington, Virginia USA

2800 Shirlington Road, Suite 1001 • Arlington, VA 22206 USA
Phone: 800-933-2723 or 703-578-9600 • Fax: 703-575-5400
Website: www.ascd.org • Email: member@ascd.org
Author guidelines: www.ascd.org/write

Penny Reinart, *Deputy Executive Director*; Genny Ostertag, *Managing Director, Book Acqui-sitions & Editing;* Mary Beth Nielsen, *Interim Director, Book Editing;* Liz Wegner, *Editor;* Thomas Lytle, *Creative Director;* Donald Ely, *Art Director;* Melissa Johnston/The Hatcher Group, *Graphic Designer;* Valerie Younkin, *Senior Production Designer;* Kelly Marshall, *Production Manager;* Shajuan Martin, *E-Publishing Specialist;* Christopher Logan, *Senior Production Specialist*

All web links in this book are correct as of the publication date below but may have become inactive or otherwise modified since that time. If you notice a deactivated or changed link, please email books@ascd.org with the words "Link Update" in the subject line. In your message, please specify the web link, the book title, and the page number on which the link appears.

PAPERBACK ISBN: 978-1-4166-3158-3   ASCD product #120024 n11/22

PDF E-BOOK ISBN: 978-1-4166-3159-0; see Books in Print for other formats.

Quantity discounts are available: email programteam@ascd.org or call 800-933-2723, ext. 5773, or 703-575-5773. For desk copies, go to www.ascd.org/deskcopy.

Library of Congress Cataloging-in-Publication Data
Names: Boix Mansilla, Veronica, author. | Jackson, Anthony (Anthony Wells), author.
Title: Educating for global competence : preparing our students to engage the world / Veronica Boix Mansilla and Anthony W. Jackson.
Description: 2nd edition. | Arlington, VA : ASCD, 2023. | Includes bibliographical references and index.
Identifiers: LCCN 2022030185 (print) | LCCN 2022030186 (ebook) | ISBN 9781416631583 (paperback) | ISBN 9781416631590 (pdf)
Subjects: LCSH: International education.
Classification: LCC LC1090 .B65 2023 (print) | LCC LC1090 (ebook) | DDC 370.116–dc23/eng/20220811
LC record available at https://lccn.loc.gov/2022030185
LC ebook record available at https://lccn.loc.gov/2022030186

32 31 30 29 28 27 26 25 24 23   1 2 3 4 5 6 7 8 9 10 11 12

Educating for GLOBAL COMPETENCE

Preparing Our Students to Engage the World

2ND EDITION

Foreword by Andreas Schleicher vii

Introduction. 1

1. A Rationale for Global Competence 7

2. Global Competence—and the Learning It Implies. 23

3. Dimension 1: Investigating the World 38

4. Dimension 2: Appreciating Perspectives 52

5. Dimension 3: Communicating Across Differences. 64

6. Dimension 4: Taking Action 74

7. Teaching for Global Competence 86

8. What Schools Can Do 104

9. Advocating Through Public Policy 123

10. What You Can Do 135

Appendix: Global Competence Matrices 142

References 155

Index. 161

About the Authors 165

Foreword

For more than three decades, globalization and digitalization have connected people across cities, countries, and continents, vastly increasing our individual and collective potential. But the same forces have also made the world more volatile, more complex, and more uncertain. We witness the growing disconnect between the infinite growth imperative and the finite resources of our planet; between the financial economy and the real economy; between the wealthy and the poor; between the concept of our gross domestic product and the well-being of people; between technology and social needs; and between governance and the perceived voicelessness of people.

Education cannot be held responsible for resolving these disconnections, but neither should anyone underestimate how people's knowledge, skills, attitudes, and values might promote social and economic development and shape the cultural context.

In today's world, education is no longer just about teaching students something, but about helping them develop a reliable compass and the tools to navigate with confidence through an increasingly complex, volatile, and uncertain world. A successful education today is one that builds curiosity (opening minds) and fosters compassion (opening hearts). It is about courage—mobilizing our cognitive, social, and emotional resources to take action. And they are also our best weapon against the biggest threats of our times: ignorance (the closed mind), hate (the closed heart), and fear (the enemy of agency).

The kinds of things that are easy to teach and test have also become easy to digitize and automate. In this age where artificial intelligence accelerates, we must think harder about what it means to be human. The future is about pairing the artificial intelligence of computers with the cognitive, social, and emotional skills and values of human beings. Today, algorithms that sort us into like-minded groups create social media echo chambers that amplify our own views and leave us insulated from opposing arguments that may alter our beliefs. These virtual bubbles homogenize opinions and polarize our societies, and they can have a significant—and adverse—impact on democratic processes.

The growing complexity of modern living, for individuals, communities, and societies, means that the solutions to our problems will also be complex. In a structurally imbalanced world, the imperative of reconciling diverse perspectives and interests, in local settings but with often global implications, means we need to become good at handling tensions and dilemmas. Striking a balance between competing demands—equity and freedom, autonomy and community, innovation and continuity, efficiency and democratic process—will rarely lead to an either/or choice or even a single solution. We need to think in a more integrated way that recognizes interconnections. Our capacity to navigate ambiguity has become key.

In today's schools, students typically learn individually, and we certify their individual achievements at the end of the school year. But the more interdependent the world becomes, the more we need great collaborators and orchestrators. We could see during this pandemic how the well-being of countries depends increasingly on people's capacity to take collective action. Schools need to help students learn to be autonomous in their thinking and develop an identity that is aware of the pluralism of modern living. At work, at home, and in the community, people will need a broad understanding of how others live in different cultures and traditions and how others think, whether as scientists or as artists.

The foundations for all this don't come naturally. We are all born with *bonding social capital*, a sense of belonging to our family or other people with shared experiences, purposes, or pursuits. But it requires deliberate and continuous efforts to create the kind of *bridging social capital* through which we can share experiences, ideas, and innovation with others, and increase our radius of trust to strangers and institutions. Getting this right is important. It will be the societies that value bridging social capital and pluralism most that can draw on the best talent from anywhere and nurture creativity and innovation.

About a decade ago, the authors of this book developed a framework for conceptualizing global competence: the capacity and disposition of individuals to see the world through different lenses, engage with different ways of thinking and working, and appreciate different perspectives and cultures. This framework inspired and organized a multitude of conversations and initiatives around the world, including the first international assessment of global competence as part of the 2018 assessment of the Programme for International Student Assessment (PISA). The findings from PISA showed that the schools and education systems that were most successful in fostering global competence were those with a curriculum that values openness to the world, that provide a positive and inclusive learning environment, and that offer opportunities to relate to people from other cultures.

But how to do this in practice? In this second edition, the authors show how the ideas of global competence can be brought to life in the classroom. The volume lays out the principles of high-quality instruction for teaching global competence and provides inspiration and ideas for educators as to what schools can do to create a culture of global competence for both students and adults.

Perhaps most important, this book not only establishes a sense of urgency for building stronger foundations for our societies but also provides the tools for how to accomplish this and a sense of optimism that this is an achievable goal, illustrated by references to the education systems that have advanced furthest on this agenda.

—Andreas Schleicher

Introduction

More than a decade ago, we were completing the manuscript for *Educating for Global Competence: Preparing Our Youth to Engage the World* (2011). At the time, the world was calling on educators to become more globally conscious, to become more aware of our growing interdependence and mutual obligations within and beyond national borders. Accelerated flows of people, ideas, products, and capital the world over demanded that we address global issues with a broader transnational scope and that we come to understand our lives, communities, and nations in terms of dynamic global interaction.

Today, a little over 10 years later, we complete this second edition, writing from our homes. COVID-19 has put our global interdependence on full display—witness the mask-covered faces, sanitized hands, heartbreaking news streams, distanced human interactions, and the hopes and fears associated with new vaccines. The pandemic has shed light on unfathomable loss, harrowing inequities, and systemic forms of exclusion around the world that leave no one untouched. We find democratic institutions in need of repair and environmental vulnerabilities in need of attention, and we're hearing a call for renewed visions about the role of education in constructing more sustainable, inclusive, and just societies.

COVID-19 has also shed light on the tireless commitment of millions of educators the world over who learned how to teach online at unprecedented speed, embrace their students more fully, and connect with families and cultural institutions. Educators worked to deliver on the promise of the right to education, even under the most strenuous circumstances. In so doing, they also strengthened our future. COVID-19 is not the first nor will it be the last chapter in the story of our global interdependence as a species. This is why we approach the second edition of our book acknowledging the wonderous journey of the ideas we published then, while keeping our gaze on the future.

In our first edition, we drew on the work of the dynamic Global Competence Taskforce at the Council of Chief State School Officers led by Tony and the Asia Society. We articulated and illustrated our framework for global competence using research on high-quality interdisciplinary and global education led by Veronica at the Harvard Graduate School of Education. The book brought together exemplary cases of learning and teaching for global competence led by teachers working with diverse populations of students around the world. The first edition was distributed broadly in digital form, reaching the hands of school leaders, teachers, students, teacher educators, policymakers, and philanthropists.

Looking back, perhaps the brightest and most humbling consequence of this work has been its power to ground public conversations about the purpose of education in a globally interdependent world. For some, the book was a reminder of a rapidly changing global stage and the need to rethink what and how we teach. Others resonated with the four dimensions of the framework: how to nurture the capacity to investigate the world beyond one's immediate environment, how to understand perspectives other than one's own, how to communicate across differences, and how to take action to improve conditions. Still others saw an invitation to trust our young to tackle complex and ill-defined issues with the support of powerful pedagogies. And some saw an opportunity to broaden their role as transmitters of fixed information to become inquirers of the most pressing issues of our times.

Frameworks have an orienting function; they enable us to "see better" by highlighting valuable dimensions. They also offer a common platform and language for exchange across disciplines, educational levels, and institutions. In fact, frameworks gain their meaning through dialogue. For example, the meaning we attribute to *perspective taking* in our classrooms is typically infused with values and permeated by culture, institutions, and geopolitical perspectives. The ongoing reinterpretations of and dialogue about global competence that our framework has engendered have enabled us to detect its blind spots and increase its nuance.

The last decade has seen a proliferation of new sister frameworks that foreground qualities such as empathy, bilingualism, whole-school reform, cultural grounding, and teacher development, to name a few. In the meantime, educators and both district and state leaders across the United States and abroad have progressively turned to teaching for global competence. More recently, at the Organisation for Economic Co-operation and Development (OECD), Veronica co-led with a group of experts on intercultural learning, citizenship education, learning and policy analysis, and teacher education the advancement of an integrative OECD global competence framework. Tony and his colleagues at the Asia Society worked to align our original framework with this newer, integrative one.

For this second edition of the book, we have chosen to feature the OECD framework, not only because of its clear continuities with our previous work, but also and more important because it captures lessons learned over the last few years. For instance, the framework foregrounds *a whole-person view of learning* as cognitive, socioemotional, and civic. It articulates the purpose of global education as *the construction of more inclusive and sustainable societies*. We also value the framework's international standing and its utility in informing decision making from the classroom to the educational boardroom. This framework can serve as a shared platform for deliberation about how to prepare our youth to live and thrive in a world of increasing diversity, complexity, and mobility.

As we prepare to reenter the public sphere following the multiple pandemics afflicting us—among these, viruses, economic crises, racisms, and xenophobias—we may want to see global competence as part of a larger shift unfolding in education, one that views children and adults in their full humanity, places equity and solidarity center stage, expands our sense of mutual obligation to include those we don't know around the world and in future generations, and exalts our care for the natural world.

One point is clear: Enduring shifts in education rarely emerge from peace and prosperity. Much to the contrary, they typically represent visionary education responses to historical moments of reckoning. In the United States, John Dewey's progressive education focused on the child and on their participation in and adjustment to a changing world. Dewey sought to strengthen democracy at a time when accelerated industrialization, urbanization, and immigration intersected with the Great Depression. In Italy, Loris Malaguzzi responded to the trauma of World War II with a vision of education that centered on the capable citizen-child, bearer of the right to education and able to make sense of the world in 100 languages (the infinite ways that children express their thoughts, feelings, and imaginings). The result was the long-standing tradition of the Reggio Emilia schools. In Brazil, Paulo Freire offered a *pedagogy of the oppressed* to nurture social and political consciousness in response to the wave of dictatorships that afflicted Latin America in his time.

In considering paradigmatic shifts, evolution also provides a useful lens. From an evolutionary perspective, species adapt or perish. For humans, the locus of adaptability has shifted over time from physical capacities to mental capacities. Put simply, nowadays human survival depends on how we act *based on how we think*. This evolutionary fact places the education of our young at center stage in ensuring cultural and environmental survival.

And how *do* we humans think, in fact? There are two competing worldviews here. The *dominance paradigm* assumes that in the natural order of things, there are winners and losers. Some people are stronger, smarter, faster, or more capable of achieving hegemony over others. In the dominance paradigm, it is legitimate for them to do so; it's just the way things are and have always been.

The competing worldview, *the egalitarian paradigm*, recognizes that people and societies differ in profound ways but that these differences do not require or legitimize the dominance of one person over another or one group over another. Instead, we consider others as being on the same level as ourselves, equally deserving of that which enables anyone to survive and thrive.

Educating for global competence means that we must educate all youth to develop this more egalitarian mindset. If we are to root out racism and survive as a species, education in the United States and on a global scale must develop in youth the disposition to act more toward the common good than toward individual gain or group hegemony.

Of course, new educational paradigms are never the result of a single book or a single mind. Instead, they emerge through the generative disruptions of ideas, practices, and tools that often challenge the status quo. We hope that this second edition of *Educating for Global Competence: Preparing Our Students to Engage the World* will contribute, along with other perspectives, to inform the more inclusive, equitable, and sustainable global education we need.

This book is intended for classroom teachers, administrators, informal educators, policymakers, community leaders, researchers, parents, students, and all other stakeholders interested in preparing our youth for the 21st century. We define *global competence* as the capacity to examine local, global, and intercultural issues; understand and appreciate the perspectives and worldviews of others; engage in open, appropriate, and effective interactions with people from different cultures; and act for collective well-being and sustainable development (OECD, 2018).

Globally competent individuals are aware, curious, and interested in learning about the world and how it works. They can use the big ideas, tools, methods, and languages that are central to any discipline (mathematics, literature, history, science, the arts) to engage the pressing issues of our time. Foundational to global competence ethics is an egalitarian model that deeply appreciates diversity and human dignity and prioritizes the common good.

Becoming better at educating for global competence involves rethinking practices and recognizing that there are no simple recipes for success. So use this book flexibly. Browse, make connections, and concentrate on the chapters that you find most pertinent to your work. Experiment with ideas, challenge concepts, and share with colleagues. Ultimately, this book must work for you. Read it in a way that best meets your needs, inspires your curiosity, and proves fruitful in the classroom.

A Look at the Book

Chapter 1 offers a rationale for global education; it outlines what has changed over the last decade and why we need human-centered global education now more than ever. Chapter 2 introduces the conceptual framework for global competence, discusses its application in the 2018 Programme for International Student Assessment (PISA), and explains the key role of disciplinary and interdisciplinary foundations in student learning. Chapters 3–6 focus, respectively, on the four core capacities associated with global competence: examining local, global, and intercultural issues; understanding and appreciating perspectives; engaging in open, appropriate, and effective interactions across cultures; and acting for collective well-being and sustainable development. Chapter 7 considers core principles of high-quality instruction for teaching global competence, illustrating them with a unit on climate change. Chapter 8 looks at what schools and educational institutions can do to promote global competence and how they might create a culture of global competence for both students and adults. Chapter 9 places global competence in the larger framework of public education systems in and beyond the United States, illustrating what countries like Singapore and Canada have done to ensure that all students are prepared for the world. Chapter 10 concludes with a call for action and outlines how multiple stakeholders can leverage their influence.

We hope this book will inspire readers to contribute to a more human, kinder, more inclusive, and more global educational model that takes to heart the question, What kinds of societies do we seek?—one that views the daily educational practice in our schools, cultural institutions, families, and communities as pivotal in the construction of a shared future.

A Rationale for
Global Competence

Not long ago, globalization—the accelerating traffic of goods, ideas, people, and capital around the world (Coatsworth, 2004)—reigned in the collective imagination as the thrust propelling the new "small," "connected," "flat" world of the 21st century. Previous 20th century assumptions about the world were rapidly becoming obsolete. For many, it became clear that a new wave of global movement of goods, capital, and labor, combined with the digital revolution, mass migratory flows, and the prospect of climate instability, were shaping societies and demanding a new kind of graduate. At a premium was a young person able to thrive in this new global platform, participate in emerging global labor markets, navigate increasingly diverse neighborhoods, and operate within fast-growing digital connectivity.

Today, as we look out into the world from the windows of our unequal homes and conditions, COVID-19 is drastically reshaping our patterns of interaction. Restrictions in movement, social distancing, and the unimaginable loss of lives are giving rise to yet another chapter in the human story of our global interdependence as a species. The rapid global spread of the virus is confirming that what happens on one side of our small planet has a direct effect on those who live on the other side. Most telling, the virus spread has shown our human propensity for xenophobia when under stress.

Global Interdependence: The Fears and the Hopes

Today our global interdependence is a matter of fact as well as contention. Daily consumption patterns in Los Angeles or Beijing influence the lives of people and ecosystems across the world. A stubborn drought in the Syrian countryside steers thousands to the city of Damascus, where a volatile political scenario soon becomes ground zero for global powers' arm-wrestling aspirations to lead on the world stage. As a result, millions of men, women, and children are forced into the life vests and life rafts that will—if successful—deliver them on the shores of a new life. Their arrival initiates a hopeful reinvention of the self, accompanied by newfound stigma and invisibility. In turn, economic discontent, especially among low-income workers in developed countries, paired with digital connectivity, xenophobic anxieties, and the emergence of fake news, trigger robust waves of nationalist and nativist movements.

The voices vary. Some demand a slowdown of the transnational integration of the last decades in favor of cultural preservation and sustainable lifestyles. Others have taken a more radical, anti-global turn by demanding a sharp reversal of transnational integration, thus feeding the flames of xenophobic othering—a nationalist "us" versus "them" mentality—at home and abroad. These voices are transforming the global political arena, redrawing alliances, slowing global manufacturing, and erecting new symbolic and physical walls. Nationalism and xenophobia are global phenomena (Harari, 2018).

The world has entered the third decade of the 21st century with sobering lessons learned. Early globalization's perceived promise of continuous economic growth and democratizing connectivity, rooted in open trade and investment liberalization, yielded increased production and a wealthier world but left many behind. New patterns of global consumption emerged the world over, with a welcomed rise of the middle class in the developing world. But the newly expanded consumption also accentuated global environmental risks (increased greenhouse gases, droughts, floods, sea level rise), threatening the very sources of livelihood on which we depend and placing our most vulnerable communities at the greatest peril (such as coastal populations and farmers in the Global South). Although unprecedented global digital connectivity has enabled us to access world events and remain in touch with friends and loved ones around the world, it has also given rise to heightened in-group/out-group online dynamics, cyberbullying, and the viral spread of fake news. Anxieties about an uncertain future, growing distrust in governing institutions, and the rise of uncivil public discourse are increasingly characterizing the world that our children are growing up in.

However, not all the news is somber. Responding to the global pandemic, teachers have embraced digital innovations on an unprecedented scale, setting the stage for new conversations about the future of learning and the interdependence of schools, families, and cultural institutions in raising the whole child. We have also witnessed a welcomed call for more inclusive economic growth (OECD, 2018), more attention to societal well-being, more humane concern for migrants on the move, a greater commitment to environmental preservation, and a greater focus on reducing inequalities. That is, we have glimpsed a kinder, more responsible form of global interdependence.

Nowhere is this hopeful international effort more vivid than in the attention the world has given to the United Nations' Sustainable Development Goals, a collection of 17 global goals for 2030, ranging from eliminating poverty and hunger to combating climate change; ensuring sustainable water management and sanitation for all; and making human settlements inclusive, safe, and resilient. Collectively, these goals set out a "blueprint to achieve a better and more sustainable future for all" (United Nations, 2020a), itself an exciting foundation for a relevant curriculum. Here, too, education plays a pivotal role in achieving these goals in the generations to come, as Goal 4, Target 4.7 indicates:

> By 2030, ensure that all learners acquire the knowledge and skills needed to promote sustainable development, including, among others, through education for sustainable development and sustainable lifestyles, human rights, gender equality, promotion of a culture of peace and non-violence, global citizenship and appreciation of cultural diversity and of culture's contribution to sustainable development. (United Nations, 2020b)

To effectively prepare our youth for the world, educators must identify key skills, values, and attitudes worth cultivating. In response, the OECD gathered the input of expert leading policymakers and practitioners from around the world to advance a new framework for global competence education. An accompanying international global competence PISA assessment (OECD, 2020) was designed to take the temperature of current global competence capacities among young people (age 15), as well as gauge the ways in which schools across participating countries are supporting their growth.

What we need for these times is a recalibrated vision of global competence as an aspiration for all youth. This vision recognizes the role of values such as human dignity, inclusivity, equity, and sustainability as central to a globally informed education that simultaneously fosters students' cognitive, socioemotional, ethical, and civic development (Boix Mansilla, 2018). A high-quality education for global competence is not a luxury destined for privileged youth. Rather, we need to ensure it reaches our most vulnerable families, children, and youth, helping them understand the increasingly complex, dynamic, and diverse world in which they live and the local and global dynamics shaping their lives and futures.

The Forces That Shape Us

Four forces shape our lives and set a new stage for our educational efforts: accelerated global migration flows and changing demographics; climate instability and the call for sustainable forms of life; the radical transformations wrought by digital technologies; and the ongoing demands of rapidly changing labor markets, calling for human capacities that resist automatization. Let's look at each of these and the competences they call for.

Preparing Students for a World on the Move

International migration is reaching historic dimensions, changing the demographics of classrooms and neighborhoods alike. According to data from the *World Migration Report 2022* (McAuliffe & Triandafyllidou, 2021), the number of international migrants worldwide was nearly 281 million, or 3.6 percent of the world's population, in 2020—up from 221 million in 2010. Europe and Asia hosted around 87 and 86 million international migrants, respectively, which counts as 61 percent of the international migrant population. These regions were followed by North America at 21 percent (almost 59 million in 2020), Africa at 9 percent,

Latin America and the Caribbean at 5 percent, and Oceania at 3 percent. No region of the world remained untouched by migratory flows (United Nations, 2019), which suggests that migration, diversity, and hybridity are rapidly becoming the norm rather than the exception.

Although most international migrants integrate into their new society relatively safely over time (Waters, 2007), an extraordinary number of people (more than 100 million in 2022) are forcibly displaced, fleeing persecution, conflict, violence, and environmental degradation (USA for UNHCR, 2022). Together with unchecked climate change, the precarious situation of refugees, asylum seekers, and internally displaced human beings represents the most jarring humanitarian crisis our world has seen in decades. These tragic developments raise essential questions about responsibility—about the role of the state, international institutions, civil society, and individuals in guaranteeing basic human rights for all. They also call on educators to renew their efforts to foster young people's capacity to build inclusive societies, uphold the universal values of human dignity and respect for diversity, and expand their circles of influence.

Ample evidence points to the economic contribution of migrants in their countries of both origin and destination. In 2019, the migrant population was responsible for approximately $550 billion in remittances back to their countries of origin, which represents a growing percentage of these countries' gross domestic product (GDP) and a total sum larger than foreign direct investment, contributing to reducing economic inequalities primarily in the North-South axis (United Nations, 2019).

Contribution and remittances are not solely economic (Levitt & Lamba, 2009). In fact, thanks to accessible digital connectivity, we now see the emergence of *transnational* migrants. Unlike migrants in previous generations, these individuals are likely to remain in close contact with their countries of origin. They participate in religious, economic, cultural, and often political activity in two places, which enables them to take multiple perspectives and adjust their own as a matter of course. For these relatively globally competent youth, healthy adaptation involves the development of a hybrid identity and dual forms of citizenship and belonging that resist having to choose one nation or community over another (Suárez-Orozco, 2001; Suárez-Orozco et al., 2008). The hybrid identities developed are reminiscent of the *double consciousness* first described by W. E. B. Du Bois in *The Souls of Black Folk* over a century ago.

> The history of the American Negro is the history of this strife—this longing to attain self-conscious manhood, to merge his double self in a better and truer self. In this merging he wishes neither of his older selves to be lost.... He simply wishes to make it possible for a man to be both a Negro and an American, without being cursed and spit upon by his fellows, without having the doors of Opportunity closed roughly in his face. (2007, p. 9)

These circumstances present educators with a powerful opportunity to view the classroom as a site of global competence development. Today, in postindustrial societies, more than a quarter of children under the age of 18 have an immigrant parent. In the United States, the proportion is expected to rise to a third by 2050 (Pew Hispanic Center, 2013). These students bring important cultural, linguistic, and relational assets to their new schools, as well as the capacity to straddle cultures. In today's contentious political climate about migration, these children are also experiencing multiple forms of exclusion and trauma (Rogers et al., 2019).

With all this in mind, how can we best prepare young people for a world in which diversity, movement, cultural exchange, and hybridity are the new normal? In other words, how can we nurture the global competence dispositions needed to advance inclusive and welcoming societies?

The competences students need to flourish in a world of migration. Preparing our youth to participate successfully in a diverse world requires providing them with multiple opportunities to experience and reflect on what happens when people from different cultures meet, whether in their neighborhood, classroom, or virtually. We need to come to understand migration as a shared human experience past, present, and future (Boix Mansilla, 2018; Re-imagining Migration, 2021). Students need to be able to appreciate the perspectives and worldviews of others as well as their own and engage in open, appropriate, and effective relationships, communicating across cultural, religious, linguistic, and personal differences (Appiah, 2008; Kymlicka, 1995; UNESCO, 2007).

Globally competent individuals can examine and explain their own worldviews and cultural traditions, recognizing how these influence their choices and interactions in everyday life. Such individuals can also weigh others' perspectives, considering the factors—such as culture, geography, religion, and so on—that inform them. They feel empathy for other people's experiences, are inclined to understand their point of view, are compassionate, and feel moved to support others (Suarez, 2003; Zaki, 2019). Students will also need to understand what happens when cultures meet and influence one another and how differences in power, wealth, and access to knowledge affect opportunities for individuals and social groups. Thriving in a world of diversity involves communicating with diverse audiences and being able to recognize how different audiences may interpret information informed by their own perspectives. Students must know how to listen and communicate openly, carefully, and respectfully, using appropriate languages and technologies to do so.

If recognizing perspectives and communicating and building relationships across difference are at the heart of students' preparation for an interactive world, two other competences—investigating global issues and taking action—are of no lesser value. Students who are able to pose their own questions and investigate cultural interactions are more likely to reflect on the complexities they present. And students who are able to envision and carry out a plan of action—perhaps to aid cultural dialogue through community service or raise awareness about different perspectives through an art exhibit or blog—come to view themselves as welcoming contributors in an increasingly diverse world.

Clearly, these tasks are not the sole responsibility of social studies teachers. It behooves art, mathematics, science, language, and second language teachers to renew their curricula as well. In fact, it behooves the whole school to create a climate that highlights these capacities and fosters their growth in adults and children alike (Bennet, 2009; British Council, 2013; Deardorff, 2009; Deardorff & Bowman, 2011; Seelye, 1996).

Preparing Students for Environmental Stewardship

Scientists around the world continue to document climate change, as well as rising temperatures in our oceans and the atmosphere. Global warming is too narrow a term to describe a phenomenon that is shaping life on the planet, affecting the earth's climate, chemistry, and biology simultaneously (Sachs, 2008).

Consider a few of the consequences. Over the last few decades, the earth has experienced a rise in the frequency and intensity of extreme weather events. Ocean levels are rising due to thermal expansion and the melting of polar ice sheets, affecting coastal areas and their water supply. Climate and chemistry changes are affecting land and sea habitats, causing large-scale extinction. Infectious diseases like malaria have already spread as rising temperatures make new regions accessible to the mosquitoes that transmit the disease. Rising temperatures and shifting patterns of precipitation are also affecting agricultural productivity (Sachs, 2008). As a research brief on climate change puts it,

> Much of the nation's experience to date in managing and protecting its people, resources, and infrastructure is based on the historic record of climate variability during a period of relatively stable climate. Adaptation to climate change calls for a new paradigm—one that considers a range of possible future climate conditions and associated impacts, some well outside the realm of past experience. (National Research Council, 2010, p. 1)

Responding to the potential impacts of climate change and limiting warming to 1.5 degrees centigrade as proposed by the Paris Agreement entail understanding not only the science underlying this pressing global phenomenon, but also the ethics of unequal distribution of the burden of climate change across generations (today's adults and tomorrow's youth) and across regions (post-industrial and developing countries). Recognizing such inequalities and developing the capacities to respond to them will prepare subsequent generations to more effectively manage the consequences of climate change, including a massive increase in the numbers of climate refugees.

Because greenhouse gases do not respect national borders, the problem is essentially a global one. Climate change is affecting every region, country, city, and village on the planet in distinct ways and shaping living conditions, job opportunities, and civic participation for youth. Over the last decade, the search for increased energy efficiency has triggered new industries and technologies—from green architecture to carbon sequestration tools. Political life the world over has seen a rise in environmental debates; in fact, the environment is reported to be a primary motivator for youth civic participation in industrialized countries, as has been powerfully illustrated by Swedish climate activist Greta Thunberg, who has inspired young people around the world to protest inadequate government action on the crisis (Haste, 2007).

It will take concerted global efforts to return atmospheric temperatures to sustainable levels. Mitigating and adapting to change will require furthering international climate agreements and enlisting all sectors of world societies in prudent resource use and sustainable innovation (Sachs, 2008). A comparative advantage will go to those who, based on a deep understanding of the problem, can create novel solutions. However, progress will not stem solely from the newest technology or the latest top-level multilateral agreement; it will pivot on the numberless private decisions of individuals who view themselves as agents of history and as globally competent actors in today's world.

The competences students need to flourish in a world of climate instability. Such preparation may begin by engaging the young with nature in positive and loving ways (Boix Mansilla & Schleicher, 2022), with the understanding that we share a single planet. This is especially important at a time when students have fewer opportunities in and out of school to interact directly with nature. In the United States, for example, students ages 8–12 use digital media an average of 5.5 hours a day while their 13- to 18-year-old counterparts do so up to 8.5 hours (Rideout et al., 2022). Given the extreme weather reports in the news and students' limited connections to nature, it's not surprising that young people may increasingly view nature as a threatening place (Louv, 2011).

Preparing youth as global environmental stewards also implies helping them understand the workings of the earth, human population growth, why and how climate change both past and present takes place, and its consequences on various habitats and ecosystems, including their own. It requires that students understand how energy consumption in one place affects the living conditions of people on the other side of the world and how we all depend on the same atmosphere for life.

Well-prepared individuals will be able to *investigate* climate change sources and effects, framing local problems for study, collecting and interpreting data, and building informed arguments. Most important, these individuals will need to understand that scientific claims and projections are empirically grounded interpretations of the problem and that today's knowledge may be legitimately revised when new and more compelling frameworks or evidence become available. These individuals will need to see that our understanding of climate is provisional and subject to critique—and view these qualities as markers of strength, not weakness.

The global nature of climate change will demand that students learn to *recognize perspectives* carefully. How does a rising ocean affect fishing populations in Alaska or in coastal tourist villages in Bangladesh and New England? Are communities prepared to face the challenge? What adaptation options do they have? Thinking about climate change in ways that consider multiple locations, perspectives, and concerns and *communicating* effectively about these conditions prepare students for transnational cooperation—the kind of global approach necessary to mitigate and adapt to climate change. Individuals who understand environmental systems around the world will be at a premium. In addition, such individuals will find opportunities to *act* now as global environmental stewards.

Perhaps most important, preparing our young for a world of climate instability isn't merely the task of science or mathematics teachers who can teach students how to examine data, reason with evidence, and consider perspectives as well as probabilistic scenarios. It entails a broader thrust toward strengthening the values around human dignity and cultural diversity that will enable more informed decision making.

Preparing Students for Unprecedented Digital Global Connectivity

Over the last two decades, we have seen radical transformations in digital technologies. Online networks, social media, and interactive technologies are leading to new learning styles in which students exercise a greater control over what and how they learn (OECD, 2018). At the same time, the digital life of young people is not only affecting their connection with their self and the world, but also influencing their actions on others. In fact, online behavior suggests that young people tend to flock together (Zuckerman, 2013), favoring interactions with a small set of people with whom they have much in common.

In recent years, the presence of fake news, paired with insufficient media literacy on the part of students, has complicated the process of distinguishing fact from fiction. Drawing on a nationally representative sample of high school students, the Stanford History Project and colleagues (Breakstone et al., 2019) found that the majority of the students believed a fake video related to the 2016 U.S. Democratic presidential primaries (the video was actually shot in Russia); few students actually tracked down the source of the video. Two-thirds of students could not distinguish between an ad and news. And 96 percent were unable to assess the credibility of a website. The researchers warned that

> A polluted information supply imperils our nation's civic health. We need high-quality digital literacy curricula, validated by rigorous research, to guarantee the vitality of American democracy. (p. 3)

A number of researchers have explored the promises and perils of ubiquitous access to technology among youth. Leading the MacArthur research network on Digital Media and Learning, Mimi Ito and colleagues (2013) have proposed a new connected learning model in which children and youth learn ubiquitously around the clock in digital spaces in and out of school with peers; such learning is informed by their interests and their academic and career aspirations and is fashioned by their agency and choice. In turn, scholars such as Sheryl Turkle (2011), Carrie James (2014), and Howard Gardner and Katie Davis (2013) have all written about the various dimensions of digital life, addressing the social and ethical dilemmas of isolation, privacy, property, and participation. Responding to the need for more informed and critical participation in digital life, organizations ranging from Google to the MacArthur Foundation and the Stanford History Education Group are developing curricula, tools, and methods to teach digital safety and responsible citizenship.

The competences students need to flourish in the digital age. Global competence education involves preparing students to navigate information sources critically, consider multiple perspectives, and employ sourcing heuristics that might prevent them from being fooled by partisan, biased, or fake news. Prepared in this way, students will be more apt to use digital spaces to truly understand the world in which they live, appropriately voice their opinions, and engage responsibly online as ethical, global, and digital citizens (James, 2014; Kahne et al., 2015).

In addition to becoming more savvy about spotting misinformation, students will need to broaden their searches to include international sources and perspectives and manage translations of pertinent material. They will need to be aware of participation bias—that is, the illusion that what a few highly active internet users do or post represents a majority position. Similarly, students will need to exercise care in sharing their own or others' information, ensuring that they don't disseminate private information, sensitive images, or unfounded perspectives.

Our digital world also enables our young to engage with different cultures. Over the last few decades and accelerated by COVID-19, digital cultural exchange programs have continued to grow (Stevens Initiative, 2020). For example, one program in the initiative has participants in the United States, Jordan, and Iraq virtually discuss solutions to the 17 Sustainable Development Goals set forth by the United Nations. Scholars have found that such programs can help young people feel comfortable when interacting with those from different cultures and foster empathy and perspective taking.

The digital world presents novel challenges and opportunities for social interaction. Social cues are less clear to read online, and anonymity can distort perceptions and facilitate harm to self and others. At the same time, the internet can amplify kindness. As Google's (2019) "Be Internet Awesome" curriculum puts forth,

> Learning to express kindness and empathy—and how to respond to negativity and harassment—is essential for building healthy relationships and reducing feelings of isolation that sometimes lead to bullying, depression, academic struggles, and other problems.

Finally, preparation for the digital world will require that students learn to participate online with civility and understanding, seeking support when needed and being brave enough to speak up about or report any misuse of digital tools.

Preparing Students for the New Global Economy

Consider the changing face of the business world. A company in one country employs workers in another, and consumers in a third country buy the goods produced. Transactions are aided by high-speed internet communication, the lowering of import tariffs, and government incentives for foreign investment. The result is a process of transnational production and exchange that has become a matter of course even through ebbs and flows of national interests and varying open trade policies. In the workplace, teams are increasingly diverse. Employers are looking for competent individuals who are able to communicate and work across differences both online and off. Well-being in the workplace depends on workers' capacity to understand and communicate with one another, upholding the values of dignity, egalitarianism, and respect.

Now a new distribution of labor is in the making. Jobs that involve routinized tasks or scripted responses will increasingly be done by computers; machines are replacing assembly line workers, bank tellers, receptionists, and travel agents, and they're increasingly taking on simple "interaction work." In contrast, jobs that demand expert thinking and complex communication will remain in growing demand. Employers will prize candidates who can collaborate with people from multiple cultural backgrounds, build trust in diverse teams, and demonstrate empathy and respect. Developing such competences is of the essence as educational systems respond to chronic youth unemployment, which has risen sharply since the 2008 recession. As a McKenzie Global Institute report (Manyika et al., 2012) put it,

> Young people who leave school without the skills they need to be hired or who never land an entry-level job where they can acquire skills suffer lifelong learning handicaps and are more likely to require social services. (p. 9)

At the beginning of the 20th century, only 5 percent of the jobs in the United States required specialized knowledge and skill. By the year 2009, at least 70 percent did, with those percentages continuing to rise (National Center on Education and the Economy, 2008). For example, a Pew Research Center report (2016) on the state of American jobs shows that jobs requiring average or above-average levels of social skills increased 83 percent from 1980 to 2015. Similarly, jobs requiring higher levels of analytical skills increased 77 percent during that same time period. The jobs of chief executives, civil engineers, postsecondary teachers, and nurses all require such higher-level skills, whereas jobs requiring higher levels of physical skills, such as machinery operation or tool manipulation skills (carpenters, welders, and the like), increased only 18 percent.

Commentators such as Daniel Pink have pointed to the emergence of a *conceptual age* that requires more than specialized skills and basic information. Our age demands workers who are able to synthesize different types of information creatively (Gardner, 2009). In fact, the New Commission on the Skills of the American Workforce (National Center on Education and the Economy, 2008) postulates that the key to successful participation in the new global labor market is a

> deep vein of creativity that is constantly renewing itself and...a myriad of people who can imagine how people can use things that have been never available before, create ingenious marketing and sales campaigns, build furniture, write books, make movies, and imagine new kinds of software that will capture people's imagination and become indispensable to millions. (p. 3)

The competences students need to flourish in the global economy. Multiple skill sets have been proposed as essential to prepare our future workforce (Levy & Murnane, 2004). They range from thinking creatively and using systems thinking to skills associated with life and careers, such as designing, evaluating, and managing one's work. Surprisingly absent in public discourse about work readiness is the need for deep understanding of issues of global significance—how global markets operate, the promise and perils of transnational production, how social entrepreneurs contribute to human development while also meeting their bottom line, the demands of economic and cultural development, and the dilemmas of inequality, to name a few.

For example, what responses to mitigating the spread of COVID-19 around the world have been most effective and why? How are crops responding to climate change in different regions of the world, and how have farmers responded? What are the economic and social consequences of protectionism in international trade? What tools do individuals, communities, and nations have to promote economic development and eradicate extreme poverty? Engaging complex questions of this kind can encourage students to *understand and appreciate perspectives and worldviews,* their own and others', and give them ample opportunities to learn to *communicate and interact* across differences—two additional capacities that are especially important in today's global work teams. Most important, preparing to work in a new global economy will require students to *take reflective action.* For example, students might design

and promote products to succeed in a digital world or develop an awareness campaign about the environmental consequences of their city's
purchasing habits.

Efficiency, productivity, and innovation capacities are important for
young people as they enter the new global labor markets. But it's equally
important to strengthen their cognitive and socioemotional capacities,
as well as their ethical and civic core, inviting them to assess both the
immediate and far-reaching consequences of their labor and to find
ways to meet the bottom line while, at the same time, contributing sustainable and humane solutions.

In Sum

The consensus is clear. The world for which we are preparing our youth
is qualitatively different from the industrial world in which school systems the world over were created. Over the last decades, numerous
reports and policy statements have emphasized the need for new skills
for the 21st century. More recently, the Council of Europe (2016) has
advanced a framework and series of recommendations to place competences for democratic cultures at the center of our educational efforts.
This work views democracy as a key mission of education systems and
the capacity for intercultural dialogue as an essential component for success. Informed by our work on global competence education at the Asia
Society and Harvard Project Zero, as well as by the Council of Europe's
work on Democratic Citizenship, the OECD framework for global competence recognizes the central role that global interdependence will play
in the lives of our youth.

Today, countries hold different views on the meaning and value of
democracy. For some of us, democracy is a shared aspiration that, even
if it's imperfect, underlies our ongoing efforts to "perfect our union." For
others, *democracy* like *freedom* connotes an externally imposed mandate
of a West perceived as distant and viewed with suspicion. Regardless of
where we stand on the geopolitical map, values of human dignity and
appreciation for diversity are of the essence if we are to nurture our
youth for a kinder world.

To achieve this goal, educators must go beyond identifying target
skills generically defined. We propose a framework that puts needed
skills to the service of nurturing every young person's human potential

and advancing more inclusive and sustainable societies. Such a framework views students as prioritizing *the kind of person the student might become* (Boix Mansilla, 2016, 2017).

The OECD definition of global competence echoes these aspirations. It does so by inviting educators to pose a more fundamental question: What matters most for students to understand about the world so they can participate fully in its future? Protecting the environment, managing unprecedented human migration, and addressing the challenges of poverty, global health, and human rights will demand a generation of individuals with a strong capacity to cooperate across national borders. The world and our youth deserve this opportunity.

Questions to Ponder

- In what ways are the societal and environmental transformations described here affecting your students' lives today? How will they affect your students in the future?

- What are key reasons for educating for global competence? What are the barriers to such an education?

- What distinguishes a high-quality education for global competence from a low-quality one?

Global Competence—
and the Learning It Implies

As we have seen, preparing our youth to fully participate in today's and tomorrow's societies demands that we nurture their global competence. But what is global competence? What kind of learning does it involve? And what does it look like at various ages and across cultures?

Defining Global Competence

In this chapter, we introduce the global competence framework developed by the OECD expert team (see Figure 2.1). The framework serves as a compass for practical decision making regarding the knowledge, skills, values, and attitudes to nurture among all youth in equitable ways.

As Figure 2.1 shows, global competence is a dynamic and multifaceted construct involving four core interrelated target capacities that students should apply in their everyday lives. This framework proposes that we nurture global competence as the capacity to

- Examine issues and situations of local, global, and cultural significance.

- Understand and appreciate different perspectives and worldviews.

- Establish positive interactions with people of different national, ethnic, religious, social, and cultural backgrounds or of different genders.

- Take constructive action toward sustainable development and collective well-being. (OECD, 2018)

Figure 2.1
The OECD Global Competence Framework

The dimensions of global competence

Source: From *Big Picture Thinking: How to Educate the Whole Person for an Interconnected World: Principles and Practices* (p. 12), by V. Boix Mansilla and A. Schleicher, 2022, OECD. Copyright 2022 by OECD.

The Four Dimensions of Global Competence

Because of the centrality of these four capacities—or dimensions—to the framework, let's now look at each of them in more depth.

Dimension 1: Examining Local, Global, and Intercultural Issues

This dimension, described in short as "investigating the world," focuses on students' capacity to investigate and understand relevant issues, be they local, national, global, or intercultural. Rather than focus on knowledge acquisition per se, it foregrounds students' capacity to apply knowledge flexibly and appropriately to novel situations. To do so, students will pair what they know with higher-order thinking skills—such as selecting, weighing, and using evidence and engaging with digital sources critically—to reason about the multiple causes of global developments or the complexities of intercultural encounters (UNESCO, 2014). This dimension invites students to produce complex explanations of local and global issues under study. It involves gathering and weighing information critically from broad sets of sources to arrive at well-grounded personal conclusions.

For instance, in a 4th grade science project designed to help students understand the effects of the ocean rising in different parts of the world, teams of students create a three-dimensional model of different coastal areas. Students then place in the model a perforated plastic bag holding ice cubes, and they wait for the ice to melt. Their goal is to model the melting of ice caps and experiment with a variety of rates and levels of ocean rising, visualizing the effect on the coastal populations they created (Boix Mansilla & Chua, 2017). In a different school, students in an 11th grade precalculus mathematics class plot population data on a graphic to examine different shapes of growth, both linear and exponential, and compare predicted years when our planet will reach carrying capacity. A 12th grade student in Mombasa, Kenya, gathers data about his peers' understanding of HIV/AIDS, comparing the views of young people across three religions: Islam, Hinduism, and Christianity. He then interviews religious leaders to understand how each tradition views the human body and disease, and he explains the differences in understanding he finds among the three groups of young people.

Dimension 2: Understanding and Appreciating the Perspectives and Worldviews of Others

As students learn about other cultures' history, values, politics, communication styles, beliefs, and practices, they begin to recognize that their own perspective is shaped by multiple influences as well, such as by their religion, gender, socioeconomic status, or education. They learn that these influences often escape conscious detection and that others have views of the world that are, at times, profoundly different from their own. Recognizing and appreciating cultural differences matter, as does forging the connections that enable us to bridge those differences and create common ground among people whose lives may have unfolded along very different paths. Such bridges might include our basic human rights and needs, common popular culture experiences, and a shared passion for music or art.

We can understand diverse perspectives even if we don't agree with those who might violate human dignity. For example, students in a 10th grade class in Shenzhen, China, explore prejudices and stereotypes that people may have toward them as new arrivals in their local communities and country. They read Martin Luther King Jr.'s "I Have a Dream" speech and compare the context and experiences of different minority groups at home and in the United States. They apply the principles that King formulated and critique stigmatization here and there. In turn, students in a 5th grade history class "step in and out" of the viewpoints of rebels and loyalists in their study of the U.S. Revolutionary War, trying to understand the conflicts that arose in supporting different sides and the complexity of such periods in history. In another classroom, a 5th grade math teacher invites students to "show their thinking and be ready to learn from their friends" as they share their solutions of a given math problem. As students point out the multiple pathways to a solution, the teacher highlights the importance of considering multiple perspectives to enrich one's thinking. She explains that a math class can be a place to practice meaningful perspective taking, something that will prepare students for an increasingly diverse world (Boix Mansilla & Wilson, 2020).

Dimension 3: Engaging in Open, Appropriate, and Effective Interactions Across Cultures

This dimension of global competence, described in short as "communicating across differences," puts a premium on high-quality communication and healthy relationships with people who may hold different viewpoints or come from different cultural backgrounds (Council of Europe, 2016). Here, students are open to multiple cultural norms, interactive styles, and degrees of formality in a given social context. This dimension calls for flexible engagement with languages and conventions, and it emphasizes appreciation for respectful dialogue and exchange.

The global competence framework proposes the capacity to interact with others across differences in ways that are open, appropriate, and effective. *Open interactions* enable students to build relationships in which all participants demonstrate sensitivity, curiosity, and a willingness to engage with others and their perspectives. In *appropriate interactions*, all participants are equally satisfied that the interaction has occurred within expected cultural norms. In *effective interactions,* all participants are able to achieve their objectives, at least in part (Deardorff, 2013).

For example, in an 8th grade classroom, students are studying the history of immigration and connecting it to contemporary migration in the United States. One student expresses frustration with "illegal aliens coming to get American jobs." An immigrant-origin classmate expresses her distress with language she feels is offensive. The teacher asks the first student, "How else could you say that and why?" employing a global thinking routine (Boix Mansilla, 2016, 2017) designed to help students become more conscious and deliberate in their language choices. Through repeated use of this routine, students develop greater autonomy in their choice of words, avoiding terms that others may find offensive.

Dimension 4: Taking Action Toward Collective Well-Being and Sustainable Development

This dimension of global competence foregrounds students' role as active members of society. From a young age, students are able to contribute to their immediate environments (school, family, and friends), as well as to more distant ones (digital spaces and places far away). This dimension recognizes that young people have multiple realms of influence and that becoming agents of change is not something to postpone for later in life (Bringle & Clayton, 2012). Taking action may imply intervening to deescalate a conflict between peers outside the school, initiating a global media campaign, disseminating a compassionate message on the refugee crisis on social media, or contributing nets to a malaria-prevention project in Kenya.

The Qualities of Essential Learning

The four dimensions of global competence offer a powerful compass to make decisions about what matters most for young people to learn. This is not about simply adding more information to an already packed curriculum. Rather, the dimensions suggest a new way to approach the content we teach, one that insists on finding opportunities for students to examine issues of local and global significance, take perspective, build or reflect on relationships across differences, and take informed and responsible actions (Klein, 2013). For example, a unit on U.S. government in the 6th grade might reference other forms of government elsewhere. Or an arts class might offer students a chance to make a portrait of an immigrant-origin peer; this would necessitate getting to know that student well enough to attempt to capture their perspective visually.

For educators to make informed decisions about how to focus our pedagogical efforts, we need to be clear about the kind of learning we seek. In fact, underlying the four dimensions are four qualities of learning on which the global competence framework is built (Boix Mansilla & Schleicher, 2022). They stem from multiple years of research on global competence pedagogies at Project Zero, carried out in close collaboration with teachers across a variety of educational levels and cultures (Boix Mansilla & Schleicher, 2022). Let's look at each of them in turn.

Learning That Engages the Whole Person

Global competence is not merely a matter of critical thinking or cognitive development; it also presents opportunities for socioemotional, ethical, and civic growth. Consider, for instance, a student who is seeking to understand why so many people leave their homes, given a world of more than 250 million international migrants. The question invites complex reasoning because, first of all, people have multiple reasons to leave; they're seeking a better life of study and work or escaping climate changes, conflict, or persecution. Second, causes are never linear; early emigrants may affect opportunities for later ones. And, finally, the decision to leave is rarely collective; parents may choose to flee against the will of children or grandparents.

At the same time, taking another's perspective in a study of human migration tends to engender empathy and compassion, as well as the ability to manage one's own emotions, essential aspects of socioemotional development. Further, as students listen to stories that new arrivals share, they encounter opportunities to deepen their values of human dignity and respect for diversity, and they practice building bridges across experiences that initially may seem too distant from their own to connect with at first sight. They begin to "see" the humanity—the power and resilience in the other—and the bridging experiences they encounter, such as friendship, love, frustration, and fear, strengthen their ethical development. This, in turn, feeds the desire to do something about the situation, to talk with a friend, to learn more, to participate in a fundraising drive or a demonstration—all essential components of students' civic development. In sum, when conceived with care and thoughtfulness, educating for global competence involves nurturing the whole child, as well as supporting the development of multiple intelligences and a student's full human potential.

Learning That Is Relevant

A global competence curriculum also calls for authenticity and relevance; it invites us to scan the contemporary world carefully to identify topics of local, global, and cultural significance (Council of Europe, 2016), such as sustainability, migration, poverty, global economic integration, and cross-cultural dialogue. This view of global competence favors issues that students are likely to encounter in their own lives, which, at the same time, might affect the lives of people around the world (e.g., a newly arriving immigrant friend at school, the origin of their T-shirts) (Perkins, 2014). Underscoring the importance of relevant learning, the OECD framework proposes four knowledge domains worthy of attention (OECD, 2018):

Cultures and intercultural relations. This knowledge domain covers such subject areas as languages, the arts, history, traditions, and norms. The world today presents ample opportunities to explore more and less successful interactions between cultural groups, as does the history of humankind. Students need to recognize inter- and intracultural differences, appreciate that we all have multiple and complex identities, and be aware of the risks of categorizing people on the basis of a single marker of identity (e.g., Black, white, female, poor). Further, by understanding differences and similarities among and within cultures and valuing cultural diversity, students are likely to become more aware of their own cultural roots and identity—another marker of personal relevance worth considering.

Socioeconomic development and interdependence. This domain focuses on the economic, technological, and social development patterns taking place in different regions of the world, as well as on the interdependences between societies and economies. Teachers can link such topics as globalization, international economic migration, consumption and transnational production, inequality, and digital connectivity to the history, social studies, or mathematics curriculum, offering students relevant opportunities to apply what they learn in class (e.g., raising awareness in school about food security and food waste practices locally and abroad, gathering and publishing stories of human migration enriching local communities). Within this domain, students learn how their daily lives are interconnected with a larger world and how local, national, and global processes shape not only the development patterns of countries, but also the opportunities that are available to them as individuals.

Environment and sustainability. Learning experiences in the domain of environmental sustainability help students understand the complex systems and policies surrounding the demand for and use of natural resources (UNESCO, 2017). This area also has abundant opportunities for action in such areas as energy consumption, smart consumption, recycling, and upcycling. Because these issues tend to figure prominently in the media, students will see that what they're learning in school is relevant to society as a whole.

Formal and informal institutions. The fourth knowledge domain of global competence focuses on institutions that contribute to our global and local governance and promote peaceful coexistence and respect of fundamental human rights. Learning about global institutions such as the United Nations, the International Criminal Court, and the World Health Organization can invite students to reflect on the forces and norms that govern a world with highly unbalanced power relationships. Students could consider how such institutions might help solve conflicts among ethnic groups or nations; manage global pandemics; or address food security, universal education, or the series of priorities established by the U.N. Sustainable Development Goals. Ideally, understanding the role of institutions will invite young people to view themselves as capable and responsible actors in society who are committed to peace, nondiscrimination, and justice and who exercise their rights in working toward those goals.

Learning That Is Deep

Globally competent students understand the earth as a system. They may be familiar with the physical landscapes of the earth and its ecosystems, the distribution of human populations, the economic resources that sustain life and growth, and their own and others' histories and cultures. These students will demonstrate deep learning not by merely *having* information about geography, historical events, or the various actors on the world stage, but by *using* such information in novel situations—to interpret a cultural conflict, explain a population pattern, or create a novel product or solution. For example, in a study of the impact of climate change on weather patterns and sea level rise in New York, South Africa, and the Seychelles islands, these students are not only able to synthesize the information they read about multiple impacts but also use this information to envision more adaptive living arrangements for local coastal communities.

In other words, deep learning calls on students to apply what they know to think flexibly about often complex and unstructured issues (Wiske, 1999). And the complex and unstructured issues that will frame the work of their generation include environmental sustainability, population growth, economic development, global conflict and cooperation, health and human development, human rights, cultural identity, and diversity (UNESCO, 2013).

Understanding these complex issues in depth demands that students apply disciplinary and interdisciplinary approaches to make sense of the world (Boix Mansilla et al., 2000; Boix Mansilla & Gardner 2006). Subjects like literature, history, economics, mathematics, biology, and the arts are powerful lenses through which to interpret the world. All too often, however, issues of local and global significance cannot be approached through a single discipline. The complex topics we've touched on all call for *interdisciplinary* approaches in that students must integrate knowledge, methods, and languages from different disciplines to solve problems, create products, produce explanations, and ask novel questions (Boix Mansilla et al., 2000; Pacheco et al., 2017).

Research on interdisciplinary education at Project Zero has identified four key features that characterize quality interdisciplinary understanding. First, interdisciplinary understanding is *purposeful*; students examine a topic to explain it in ways that would not be possible through a single discipline. Second, understanding is *grounded in disciplines*; it employs concepts, big ideas, methods, and languages from two or more disciplines in accurate and flexible ways. Third, interdisciplinary understanding is *integrative* to deepen understanding. Last, interdisciplinary understanding is *thoughtful*; students reflect on the nature of interdisciplinary work and on the limits of their own understanding (Boix Mansilla et al., 2010).

School teachers across the globe are expected to teach core sets of concepts and skills. In the United States, for example, the Common Core State Standards embody expectations for what K–12 students need to know and be able to do in areas such as English language arts and mathematics. Yet they also give teachers and schools considerable freedom to focus instruction in ways they deem significant. For example, students are required to produce a variety of texts: arguments, narratives, and explanatory texts. Yet teachers can often decide what these texts will be about. They might ask students to write a narrative on the life of a migrant child or explain how communication technologies facilitate democratic movements in a given region. By doing so, students develop their capacity to write in alignment with existing curricular expectations while simultaneously becoming more globally competent.

Learning That Is Long-Lasting

Our students spend many years of their lives with us. How might we engage them in transformative learning that stays with them over time? A focus on long-lasting learning points to the development of global competence "thinking dispositions." As our research at Project Zero suggests, these involve the *ability to examine a complex issue*, reason with evidence, take perspective, communicate reflectively, and assess courses of action. They also include the *sensitivity to opportunities in the real world* to recruit these modes of thinking in flexible and unprompted ways and an *inclination to do so* over time (Perkins et al., 2000). Dispositions are about the kind of globally minded person a student will become. They direct our educational efforts to strive for learning that is long-lasting.

Global Competence Education in Action

To illustrate how the four dimensions of global competence play out in students' learning experiences, let's look at two examples. The first one illustrates global competence education in the early years, challenging the notion that this type of education is too complex to teach to young students. The second example captures a successful global studies program for 10th graders that our research team developed more than a decade ago.

The Early Years: Faxing a Letter to Washington, D.C.

A group of 5- and 6-year-old children is brainstorming some theories on how a fax machine works; they want to know how it connects their school in the city of Reggio Emilia, Italy, to Washington, D.C. The children create drawings that build on conversations about the most efficient way to send a letter to a friend who has recently moved to the United States without using the internet. Where is the United States? What is Washington, D.C., like? Is it similar to their city?

Over the previous weeks, questions of this kind have driven the children's exploration of the globe and communication technologies. They have shared and revised hypotheses and illustrations about what their friend's school in Washington, D.C., is like, how far away the cities are from each other, and how a fax machine communicates across the ocean. How does this work illustrate students' understanding of the world? It begins with their curiosity and interest in making sense of how the world is organized spatially and how communication technologies work. The children *examine and investigate the world* beyond their immediate environment, and their drawings exhibit a beginning sense of spatial geography. The globe is not a foreign object to them, but one where they can locate themselves, their school, and their city with ease.

To decide where exactly to draw the United States and Washington, D.C., they must learn to visualize the location of continents. The children include localities that have personal meaning to them, such as the "hills of Ireland on the way to the U.S." Their intuitive representation of maps and globes will later be informed by geography. Their theories about how a fax machine works reveal their initial, if obscure, theories of technology. Such theories will be challenged toward the end of the unit when an expert visits their class to dismantle an old fax machine and explain how it works.

Students also *recognize perspectives*—theirs in Reggio Emilia and their friend's in Washington, D.C. The children's questions illustrate their budding ability to compare localities and search for similarities and differences: Is the Capitol building in Washington, D.C., like the piazza in Reggio Emilia? What animals live in the other city? What do the big buildings look like? What are schools and people like there?

Particularly compelling in this work are the nuanced and flexible ways the students put forth their emerging theories, consider others' views and solutions, revise their theories, and collaborate to understand the world. After discussing their theories, the children work together on a final group drawing. These students are not just memorizing facts or definitions, nor are they merely playing with interesting artifacts. They're engaging a complex problem in depth, communicating their thoughts collaboratively, and making sense of how the world and the fax machine work. Eventually, the students send the fax to their friend. Along the way, they've experienced the collaborative joy of discovery and the values of respect and friendship in a learning experience that has engaged and nurtured the child as a whole person.

A 10th Grade Project: Reflecting on Globalization

Every year, history teacher Michael and English teacher Joseph, together with colleagues at Newton South High School in Massachusetts, dedicate the last few weeks of class to a study of contemporary globalization. In groups, 10th graders track the production of objects that are part of their everyday life, such as Apple iPods, Motorola cell phones, Reebok sneakers, and Fender guitars. Every year, their goal is to investigate the effects, both positive and negative, that job migration has on job-receiving communities in China, India, and Mexico.

For example, a group presented on the promises and risks of building a new Reebok plant in the province of Guangdong, China. Students were charged with deciding whether or not the community should approve the plant. Three students representing corporate interests gave detailed descriptions of job opportunities, working conditions, and newly revised health standards. They emphasized the company's compliance with Articles 4 and 5 of the Universal Declaration of Human Rights—banning slavery and maltreatment—as well as their voluntarily chosen European standards for greenhouse gas emissions. They spoke of the hardships of Chinese migrant workers facing shifting values in society, and they introduced company programs to help them maintain mental and physical health.

A student representing an environmental nongovernmental organization (NGO) perspective was less optimistic about the new factory. He explained the short- and long-term consequences of deforestation on animal nutrition cycles, as well as the risk of extinction for endangered species like the giant panda and golden monkey. Other students addressed Reebok labor violations in the early 1990s—cases of child labor, compulsory overtime, and limited freedom of speech—as well as the more recent measures taken by Reebok to prevent new violations.

After complex deliberations weighing, on one hand, environmental factors and the effects on cultural traditions and, on the other, poverty elimination and job creation, the class approved the construction of the new plant but requested that local authorities develop stricter monitoring procedures (e.g., surprise visits) to enforce compliance with labor standards. Whether their teachers agreed with the students' verdict or not, one thing was clear: these students were coming to understand the difficult decisions that individuals and societies must make in a rapidly changing world.

How does this illustrate students' capacity to understand the world? Drawing from economics, the students use data about macroeconomic growth and concepts like *incentives* and *purchasing power parity* to make their case. Drawing on biology, they apply core scientific concepts, such as habitat, biodiversity, and ecological balance, to argue for the preservation of the species endangered in each region. They use skills delineated by the Common Core State Standards, such as the ability to make sense of people's lives in distant regions. They analyze relevant literary works examining the effectiveness with which authors use figurative language and rhetoric to convey the experiences of individuals confronting economic and societal change in their region. Drawing on history, students compare contemporary and historical accounts of how traditional rural families adapt during times of rapid industrialization.

Students employ curricular standards intuitively—not with the goal of preparing for a test, but because habits of mind, such as close reading of text, critical reading of data graphics, and compelling rhetoric choices, are powerful tools in understanding and acting on the problems they study. By bringing together economic, environmental, and cultural perspectives on the problems under study—that is, by doing *interdisciplinary* work—these students are better able to reason their cases with sophistication. As one 10th grader, Molly, put it,

> Globalization, in my opinion, is something that we don't have much control on. It's going to keep growing, and there's not much we can do to stop it. However, there are many things that companies, governments, and individuals can do to make it run more smoothly and get rid of some of its negative

impacts. It was essential to research the cultural, economic, political, and environmental aspects in order to not be biased (for example, if one only researched the economic part, globalization is obviously great for China when one doesn't analyze the human rights that are being violated and the environmental degradation that it's causing).

Finally, students begin to reflect on their own cultural perspectives. Explains one student, "I went right home, turned over all the dishes in my house, and found that they were all made in Malaysia. Pretty much *everything* in my house seems made in Malaysia!" She lamented knowing "almost nothing" about the people who made the dishes on which she eats. The students in this unit come to understand the ubiquitous nature of global interconnection as they see "the objects we buy at the supermarket or every plate in my home" as directly tied to the lives of the people and communities who produce them the world over. They *take action* by being more judicious in their consumption patterns, seeking to support only brands that operate responsibly in their outsourcing practices.

In Sum

Students develop global competence through whole, relevant, deep, and long-lasting learning and when they come to own the questions that guide their investigation of the world. They set out to learn not merely to pass the next quiz, but because they experience the excitement and fulfillment of coming to understand the world and their role in it. Global competence is therefore best developed within disciplinary courses or contexts. Students do not develop global competence *after* they gain fundamental disciplinary knowledge and skills, but rather *while* they are gaining such knowledge and skills. Teaching for global competence occurs in the selection of curriculum content and instructional planning that enables students to meet national and local learning standards and that gives them the opportunity to frame, analyze, communicate, and respond to issues of global significance. These capacities will certainly prepare them for increasingly demanding educational settings—including college—as well as for the worlds of work and community life.

In the next four chapters, we will be looking at each of the four dimensions of global competence learning in more depth. In the meantime, reflect on the questions that follow.

Questions to Ponder

- Take a close look at the examples of the student work provided. What qualities attract your attention? What questions do they raise? What connections can you make to your own educational practice?

- How might the four dimensions of global competence and the kind of learning we seek help you think about the knowledge and skills that your school, district, and state expect learners to master?

Dimension 1:
Investigating the World

Globally competent students are curious. They ask and explore questions like these: What is a global pandemic? Where does it come from, and how does a virus like COVID-19 pass from person to person and across regions? How does it affect people from different world regions, cultures, walks of life, and positions? What is the role of the World Health Organization in promoting global health? What is the expected effect of the COVID-19 pandemic on people's lives in my city and in other places in the world? How does the pandemic affect local economies, interactions among cultural groups, or trust in governments in, say, São Paulo, Brazil; New York; or Lagos, Nigeria?

Because global issues are typically complex, these students are less inclined to seek a preestablished "right" answer; rather, they engage intellectually and emotionally in searching for and weighing informed responses. Globally competent youth are able to identify, collect, and analyze credible information from a variety of local and international sources, including sources in languages other than their own. They navigate digital sources thoughtfully, checking the sources of claims or news, bringing healthy skepticism to what they read online. They can weigh and integrate evidence to create coherent responses and draw defensible conclusions. They can describe complex phenomena, consider multiple causes, and analyze and synthesize information (Grotzer,

2012). Their global competence becomes visible when they write an essay, design a solution, propose a scientific explanation, or create a work of art. These capacities are not demonstrated simply once but, rather, develop as long-lasting inquiries and as a critical habit of mind.

Some might consider such capacities as an impossible standard that only privileged students might attain or as something to teach only to older students. This is not the case. As American psychologist Jerome Bruner (1960) would have claimed, teachers can teach these capacities in intellectually responsible ways to children of all ages. It's important to envision what more junior versions of these capacities might be. For example, consider an early childhood classroom where children ages 3–5 are learning about the migration of Monarch butterflies from their city, Washington D.C., to Mexico. The students spend time drawing the life cycle of the butterflies they're raising in their classroom; their drawings offer concrete support for conversations about the voyage and what they know about Mexico, and they showcase the meaningful questions the students have about the butterflies' adventure.

When we look at this dimension of global competence learning—examining local, global, and intercultural issues—we see that globally competent students can

- Identify an issue, generate a question, and explain its local, global, or intercultural significance.

- Use a variety of languages and domestic, international, and digital sources critically to identify and weigh relevant evidence in addressing an issue.

- Analyze, integrate, and synthesize evidence and disciplinary insights to construct coherent, nuanced, and culturally sensitive understanding.

- Develop descriptions, explanations, interpretations, and products that are based on compelling evidence, disciplinary knowledge, and perspectives to draw defensible conclusions.

How Students Are Investigating the World

Let's now look at three projects that reveal students' growing global competence: a 12th grader's investigation in New York into Latin

American literature, a 6th grade mathematics class in Minnesota that is investigating ancient numbering systems, and a 12th grade independent research project in Mombasa, Kenya.

Learning from Latin American Literature

Gabriel García Márquez's novel *Chronicle of a Death Foretold* explores themes of family, reputation, honor, revenge, justice, obsession, and communal responsibility. Following an in-depth study of the novel, students in Ms. Wilson's 12th grade English language arts class in New York's Henry Street School for International Studies were invited to study the work of a notable Latin American poet of their choice. They had to explain their chosen writer's global significance and examine how, as in García Márquez, the author's personal experience and literary choices convey his or her unique perspective.

One student, Aliyah, focused her research on José Lezama Lima, a well-regarded and debated Cuban poet. "His writing is complicated to understand," said Aliyah, "given Lezama Lima's baroque style, [which is] similar to [that of] Luis de Góngora." In her essay, Aliyah demonstrated how Lezama Lima's work explores themes of disappointment, religion, sacrifice, and femininity. Accounts of the poet's life reveal how Lezama Lima's homosexuality and independent political views influenced his writing and his view of poets as interpreters of a complex and often paradoxical world. Aliyah wrote,

> José Lezama Lima felt alone as a child. He lived in a society that was extremely judgmental and strict. A place where communism was present...and literature was not to go against "revolutionary consciousness." [The author] was also famous for the novel he published in 1966, *Paradiso,* which is Spanish for "paradise." Because this book was detailed with content based on homosexuality, José Lezama Lima faced hardships when publishing it. According to the government, the novel went against the Cuban Revolution in that it lacked political commitment.
>
> Another source of social rejection was religion, a topic about which Lezama Lima wrote extensively. Roman Catholics do not approve of homosexuality. As a gay man, José Lezama Lima had to sacrifice his religious beliefs because he

was considered a sinner. He felt alone in social terms and in religious terms as well.

Close reading of various poems, including "Melodia," enabled Aliyah to show how Lezama Lima's experiences were reflected in his densely symbolic work. She interpreted the last lines of the poem as depicting a shattered dream, followed by a paradoxically redeeming resolution:

> Curved glass in the untwisted hand.
> Cold dart falling more refined,
> the smoke towards the flute, and desired oblivion.

> The cold darts are coming from the air.... [T]hey are targeting something—a dream. Dreams may shatter, just like glass, no matter how carefully he holds on to them. He wanted to fulfill a dream, but it vanished before he reached it: disappointment. "Melodia" evokes the many disappointments the author faced throughout his personal life as well as his career. Nevertheless, [the smoke suggests] hope will emerge, and perhaps he will unconsciously attain his desire, and his melody would be heard.... In "Melodia," Lezama Lima makes his readers envision solid objects in order [for them] to comprehend the nonliteral idea that lies within the text.

This work illustrates two ways of exercising global competence. The student did the following:

- **Identified an author and explained the local, global, and cultural significance of the author's work.** Aliyah examined universal themes within the context of the Roman Catholic and communist society in which Lezama Lima grew up. As a marginalized homosexual writer, Lezama Lima found refuge in literature and influenced a generation of Cuban writers. Aliyah's analysis of one author became an opportunity to explore the larger question of what happens when people must navigate tensions among individual, social, and cultural values and expectations.

- **Used a variety of languages and domestic and international sources to analyze, integrate, and synthesize evidence to construct a compelling argument.** To produce her essay, Aliyah had to identify, interpret, and synthesize a range of sources: original and translated publications of Lezama Lima's work, biographies, and reviews produced both in and outside Latin America. Through close reading, she discerned literary choices that both supported and challenged her argument—that is, that marginalization plays a key role in Lezama Lima's work.

In sum, Aliyah drew on literary analysis tools to make sense of the work of a poet whose life was shaped by forces very different from those shaping her own. She came to understand how this particular example of Latin American literature speaks to a specific political climate. Her learning is relevant in that it touches on local and global issues of identity, society, and expression central to Latin America. It engages her intellectually but also emotionally as she explores similarities and differences in life choices and contexts. Her learning is deep in that it's rooted in literary insights and modes of thinking. And because so much of her work involved advancing her own interpretation, the experience will yield long-lasting insights.

Investigating Ancient Number Systems

In Sandburg Middle School in Minnesota, the 6th grade math unit on ancient number systems helps students place our current decimal system in a broader global and historical context. Students are called on to recognize the diversity of ways in which humans have represented quantities and the historical innovations that contributed to the Arabic-Hindu system we use today.

To that end, a group of students did a presentation that compared two of the six ancient number systems the class explored: the Roman and Inca *quipu* systems. Three questions guided their inquiry: Which number system is better for doing computations? Which number system was more useful at the time? Which number system could we use today?

To address these questions, students tested the systems with simple mathematical operations. They also considered the number system's effectiveness in a series of tasks: keeping track of llamas in the mountains, keeping track of events over time, predicting how much wood the men in a village would be able to gather, and traveling to collect needed demographic information. They then deliberated potential uses of each number system today.

In its presentation, the group described its analytic approach. Group members measured the ease of computation according to the time it took each student to solve a given operation. They listed the pros and cons of each system and rated each system's applicability on a scale from 1 (very good) to 5 (very bad). They presented a bar graph to show how the two number systems compared. They pointed at patterns to form conclusions.

For example, Roman numbers are easy to add and subtract because they're built on a logic of addition and subtraction. In contrast, the quipu system, which consisted of carefully placed knots on a series of strings, was helpful to the Incas; because it was lightweight, it enabled them to travel along the Andes and record its population, cattle, and sheep. The portable quipu was crucial for a civilization that had not developed a written language. It also used a 10-base place value system, which made it able to handle large numbers with ease. The students also considered the disadvantages of the quipu system: the ambiguity about the meaning of particular place values on each string and the cumbersome job of having to tie knots.

This work illustrates another two ways of exercising global competence. The students did the following:

- **Investigated a topic of regional, global, and intercultural significance.** By engaging in a comparative study of number systems around the world, young students came to understand the universality of human quantitative thought and the cultural and historical variations and influences that preceded the number system we use today. By limiting their analysis to two contrasting systems, these students were able to explore the problem in depth.

- **Used a variety of languages and analyzed, integrated, and synthesized evidence to construct coherent responses.** In this unit, students explore the notational rules and forms of a variety of unfamiliar numerical languages. They gathered systematic data on the properties of systems—ease of computation, applicability to everyday life, and usefulness today—to produce conclusions that are grounded in data. In sum, the ancient number systems project engages students as whole learners. It gives them ownership of their research process, thus engaging them not only intellectually but also socioemotionally through their collaboration with peers. The project draws on mathematical reasoning appropriate for this age group, inviting deep learning. And it sheds light on the relationship between number systems and the societies around the world that created them, thus rendering mathematics and their own learning relevant.

Examining Perceptions About HIV/AIDS Across Religious Groups

As part of his essay graduation requirement for the International Baccalaureate diploma at Aga Khan Academy in Mombasa, Kenya, Raouf conducted a study of knowledge and beliefs about HIV/AIDS among three religious communities: Christians, Hindus, and Muslims. He explains that the HIV/AIDS epidemic has affected millions of families in sub-Saharan Africa, and "a missing generation of young adults has left communities unable to pull themselves out of extreme poverty." Learning about HIV/AIDS requires critically examining one's beliefs about its causes and treatments—beliefs that often intersect with cultural and religious values.

In his essay, Raouf asks two questions: What do members in each community know and believe about the causes of HIV/AIDS and its possible treatments? Do members of particular communities share similar views, and, if so, what role do religious leaders play in shaping their communities' beliefs, knowledge, and attitudes about the disease?

Raouf asked leaders, adults, and youth in the three religious communities to complete a questionnaire structured to capture popular beliefs and misconceptions about HIV/AIDS—its causes, transmission, and treatments, as well as its scientific, biological explanation. Figure 3.1 shows some of the questions he included in the questionnaire.

Results revealed consistent views within religious communities about HIV/AIDS but also important differences across them. These differences were corroborated by interviews with religious leaders, which reflected varying degrees of scientific knowledge. Building on his research, Raouf examined how religious ideas may influence communities' attitudes toward HIV/AIDS and whether those attitudes are more or less scientifically informed.

This work illustrates a student's capacity to investigate the world. Raouf did the following:

Figure 3.1

HIV/AIDS Questionnaire

1. What is HIV?
   a. A household intellectual virus
   b. A human immunodeficiency virus
   c. A human intelligence virus
   d. A humanitarian immune virus

2. How can you prevent HIV?
   i.   By staying away from infected people
   ii. By using safe blood and ensuring you don't get cut by something sharp—for example, by a nail protruding from a matatu
   iii. By not sharing utensils with infected people
   iv. By using contraceptives (condoms)
       a. i only
       b. ii and iv only
       c. i and ii only
       d. All of the above

3. Could the AIDS pandemic be avoided medically?
   a. Yes, a vaccine could be taken.
   b. Yes, people could have taken contraceptive drugs after intercourse with an infected person or bled out the blood that was transfused from an infected person.
   c. No, because the way to stop a pandemic or an epidemic is to vaccinate as many people as possible, and there is no vaccine for AIDS.
   d. No, because it's too expensive to vaccinate a whole population.

4. HIV's genetic material consists of
   a. 1 DNA strand
   b. 2 identical DNA strands
   c. 2 unidentified DNA strands
   c. 2 identical RNA strands

5. How would you behave toward a person with HIV/AIDS?
   a. Stay away from him/her.
   b. Be friendly, but avoid touching or sharing food with him/her.
   c. Behave normally with him/her, but cautious of blood exchange.
   d. Tease or bully him/her about his/her condition.

- **Identified an issue and explained its significance.** As a globally competent student, Raouf clearly explained the significance of his topic for his fellow Kenyans and other sub-Saharan Africans:

  In Kenya, in the year 2007, between 1,500,000–2,000,000 people lived with HIV/AIDS, and 85,000–130,000 people died. This means that, having affected a massive number of people, it is an area that requires a lot of awareness…. Mombasa, the area of this study, is controlled by religious ethics; mainly Islam, Christianity, and Hinduism…. [It] is important to consider that in Mombasa, religious morals and values are considered very important.

- **Used a variety of languages and domestic and international sources.** Raouf designed his survey questions to reveal scientific knowledge and misconceptions. He enriched his work by studying selected parts of sacred books from the three religious traditions. And he used language skills to produce two versions of his survey—one in English and one in Swahili, inviting subjects to choose their preference.

- **Analyzed, integrated, and synthesized evidence collected to construct a coherent response**. Raouf drew from his research to test his initial hypotheses. For example, he had hypothesized that adults across communities would not appreciate hearing religious leaders speak publicly about HIV/AIDS or sex. Yet, as he notes, the results suggest otherwise:

  > [That hypothesis was] rejected as a majority of the adult people interviewed in all three religions said that reactions to a sermon on HIV/AIDS would be positive. However, a majority of the students interviewed believed that they cannot ask questions on the matter in their religious institutions. Conversely, a number of them have heard a sermon on HIV/AIDS, which counters another hypothesis I made that the students would not have heard much in their respective religious institutions.

- **Developed an argument based on compelling evidence that considers multiple perspectives and draws defensible conclusions.** On the basis of his research, Raouf proposed the following recommendations for action:

  > The level of basic awareness was high in Aga Khan Academy throughout the year. However, in J. Academy, [awareness was low among younger groups]…. The low basic awareness in these groups could be the cause of discrimination against

people with HIV/AIDS.... These results show that although the students are aware of HIV/AIDS, they still need to be... educated mostly on the basic knowledge. This can be done in the schools by having HIV/AIDS awareness weeks, holding seminars, or even by introducing the awareness of HIV/AIDS in the syllabus of the classes. This would expose students to [the topic] and allow them to be aware of the dangers that exist.

- **Finally, Raouf showed the ability to self-critique, cautioning readers about generalizations and discussing the need for further questions for inquiry:**

[L]ooking at students in two schools is not enough to make a generalization on the level of awareness in all the international schools in Mombasa. Besides, the study did not allow students to give suggestions about what is the most effective way to raise awareness within their age mates. In the future, the same study should be repeated with all international schools in Mombasa taking part, interviewing more leaders and adults of the various sects of each religion to reach a general conclusion of what level the international schools in Mombasa are at when it comes to awareness. In addition, a similar study should be done with government schools to assist the government with raising the level of awareness in its schools.

Investigating the World: The Challenges, the Opportunities

These three examples illustrate how students can examine issues of global significance in ways that present important opportunities for them, as well as demands on them, as learners. Students come to understand that conducting research or examining a global or an intercultural issue is not merely a fact-gathering exercise, but rather a systematic effort to address and explain a meaningful phenomenon. Moving beyond simple information-gathering activities—"I will find information about Latin American poets"—students learn to frame problems that are researchable and relevant—"How did Lezama Lima's personal experience in Cuba and his literary choice influence his unique literary perspective?" Instead of posing questions that are too broad to address in depth—"Why does HIV/AIDS exist around the world?"—students learn to craft and investigate questions or frame problems that are both researchable and relevant, such as, "What do members of three religious communities in Mombasa know and believe about the causes of HIV/ AIDS and its possible treatments?"

Students who investigate and examine the world must be supported in their efforts to gather, weigh, and interpret material from a broad variety of sources—sources that often disagree. Building strong evidence-based arguments about open-ended and sometimes contentious questions is a difficult skill to acquire, but a valuable and necessary one in our changing world (Kuhn, 2008).

This also sheds light on the importance of nurturing students' sourcing and argumentation capacities. Students need to select sources purposefully to inform their understanding of the issue at hand (Reimers, 2020). They must be able to establish the reliability of a source and its relevance; understand the significance of different sources' perspectives; recognize the intentions of sources and claims and distinguish between facts, opinions, and propaganda; evaluate whether the assumptions or premises are reasonable or well-grounded in evidence; and identify assumptions or claims that reflect stereotypes. Nurturing the capacity to examine issues also requires that students recognize the provisional nature of evidence and that multiple arguments can stem from a similar set of sources.

With overwhelming amounts of information of varying quality available at their fingertips, it's especially relevant to prepare young people to navigate internet sources in informed ways. Young people often click on the first options their browsers offer during a search, disregarding whether the material is an advertisement or real or fake news. Some new and indispensable habits to develop include *vertical reading*—scanning options down the results page—and attention to sourcing. Figure 3.2 illustrates some of the cognitive developmental progressions associated with this first dimension of global competence.

Developing students' capacity to investigate the world provides innumerable opportunities to examine issues of social justice and equity. For example, in her algebra classes, one high school teacher in the United States uses newspaper stories as the starting point for brief

Figure 3.2

Examine Local, Global, and Intercultural Issues: Beginning, Learning, Mastering

	Beginning	Learning	Mastering
Selecting sources (range)	Students prefer using sources stemming from their own cultural context, without having an apparent strategy to search, select, or differentiate among sources.	Students search for and select sources stemming from geographic and cultural contexts (region, language, perspective) beyond their own. They can also search for and select more than one source type (journalistic article, publication, personal testimony, government report). No concrete strategy beyond a commitment to use different sources is apparent.	Students are able to frame the search systematically in a way that enables them to identify the nature and extent of information needed to address the issue under study. They select sources purposefully drawing on contexts and types that will inform their understanding of the issue at hand.
Weighing sources (reliability and relevance)	Students take the information at face value without considering contextual factors (author, geo-perspective, culture) or source. They cannot yet detect clear bias or inconsistencies. The students don't weigh sources' relevance vis-a-vis the topic or claim at hand.	Students weigh sources for their relevance vis-a-vis the topic or claim at hand. They also consider contextual factors that can inform their evaluation of a source's reliability. They can detect clear biases and inconsistencies, yet they show a rather binary view of reliability (biased/nonbiased).	Students pay attention to contextual factors to establish the reliability of a source and its relevance. They understand the significance of different sources' perspectives; can distinguish the communicative intentions of sources and claims (facts, opinions, propaganda); evaluate whether the assumptions or premises are reasonable or well-grounded in evidence; and identify assumptions or claims that manifest stereotypes.

(continued)

Figure 3.2—(continued)

Examine Local, Global, and Intercultural Issues: Beginning, Learning, Mastering

	Beginning	Learning	Mastering
Employing sources (reasoning with evidence)	Students view the use of sources as a simple, unproblematic matter of copying and pasting information into an argument.	Students understand the need for multiple sources but use a mechanistic approach to the inclusion of sources in an argument (e.g., two "for" and two "against" sources).	Students recognize the provisional nature of evidence and that multiple arguments can stem from a similar set of sources. They can consider evidence to explore and meet counterarguments. They can also address conflicting claims or sources.
Describing and explaining complex situations or problems	Students can produce short summaries of information or perspectives. Summaries read as a string of information with little substantive organization. Students are not yet capable of classifying the information.	Students can describe the issue/situation under study in ways that connect larger concepts (e.g., culture, identity, migration) and simple examples. They can order and prioritize content in a way that supports others' understanding of the issues.	Students can describe the issue/situation in hand in ways that connect larger concepts (e.g., culture, identity, migration) and relevant examples. They can develop and express clear, sound, and effective arguments synthesizing and connecting information provided in the task with information they acquired in or out of school.

Source: From *Preparing Our Youth for an Inclusive and Sustainable World: The OECD PISA Global Competence Framework* (p. 27), 2018, OECD. Copyright 2018 by OECD.

math-informed discussions of social justice issues. An article about the sudden spike in the price of EpiPens, which are used to reverse the effects of severe allergic reactions, inspired students to compare current prices to prices in the mid-2000s and consider whether drug makers should be allowed to charge "whatever price they want." Another teacher invited students to study the statistics behind the water quality tests of lead-tainted water in Flint, Michigan, providing an evidence base for discussion of environmental racism. "If students don't practice using math to understand the complicated issues we experience around the world now," the teacher asks, "how will they know how to do this in the future?" (Asia Society & OECD, 2018).

In classrooms that nurture global competence, students are empowered to consider issues of significance while meeting the core learning requirements (Perkins, 2009). For example, in her research on Lezama Lima, Aliyah demonstrated her developing ability to cite strong and thorough textual evidence to support her analysis of what the text says and her inferences from the text—an expected capacity for graduating students in the United States. Perhaps most important, these students have an opportunity to meet such expectations within the broader context of a meaningful investigation of their world, adding authenticity to their schooling experience and preparing them for the life of work and civic society.

Questions to Ponder

- Consider the content you're teaching this year. What specific issues of local and global significance might invite student investigation? What forms of inquiry might students learn by investigating the world?

- What are some learning challenges your students might face when framing researchable questions? When gathering, weighing, and interpreting information? When synthesizing evidence to describe or explain a phenomenon or construct a particular argument? What can you do to best support them?

- What is the value of inviting students to investigate the world beyond their immediate environment? What are the risks? Consider sharing your views with a colleague.

Dimension 2: Appreciating Perspectives

An important step that students take toward becoming more globally competent is recognizing that they hold particular perspectives on life and the world and that these perspectives and worldviews are not shared by all. Students discover that other people have other perspectives, which may or may not align with their own. Perspective taking is a cognitive, socioemotional, and ethical capacity. It involves caring for and seeking to understand oneself and others.

As students learn about other cultures' histories, languages, values, communication styles, beliefs, and practices, they come to acknowledge the many influences that shape who they are (class, gender, culture, social affiliation, education, geographic placement, religious upbringing). They learn that the multiple influences that shape their own and others' perspectives often escape conscious detection.

Students demonstrate global competence when they exhibit genuine curiosity toward other people's lives—an act that invites them to wonder about who they are and to revisit cultural assumptions they often take for granted. These students are prepared to view others with respect and empathy across differences. They wonder about others' experiences, emotional worlds, and outlook on life. They are ready to build bridges across cultural differences that are rooted in the shared human experiences of friendship, family, play, youth culture, and the like. Students who embody such dispositions are less likely to hold or internalize others' stereotypes—an essential capacity in times of rising xenophobia.

Deploying their knowledge of history, culture, and current events, students learning to become globally competent discuss their perspectives with others in ways that are mutually informative. They appreciate that cultures, languages, and traditions are neither fixed nor impermeable. They appreciate internal variation within other cultural backgrounds. They can integrate these various viewpoints to synthesize new ones—the kind of comprehensive perspective vital to learning from intercultural exchanges or developing hybrid cultural identities in the case of immigrant-origin youth.

Finally, globally competent students recognize how opportunities (such as access to knowledge and technology, health, and education) and vulnerabilities (such as the risk of catastrophic coastal flooding) are unevenly distributed in the world, affecting people's experiences, views, and quality of life.

To clarify, globally competent students do the following:

- **Recognize, value, and express their own perspective** on situations, events, issues, or phenomena and identify the influences on that perspective.

- **Understand and appreciate the perspectives of other people and groups**, seeking to identify influences on those perspectives and upholding the value of human dignity.

- **Recognize bridging connections** and explain how cultural interactions influence perspectives, situations, events, issues, or phenomena.

- **Recognize inequities in people's experiences** and how differential opportunities and vulnerabilities shape life and perspectives—others' and their own.

How Students Are Appreciating Perspectives

Let's turn to two examples that illustrate this work. The first stems from collaborative work between schools in California and Bangalore, India. The second one offers us a look at an 8th grade English language arts classroom in a Seattle public high school.

Exploring Shelters Across the World

Informed by statistics about the global rise of mega-slums and inspired by contemporary artists' engagement with such issues, the shelter project brought together students from three educational institutions. Two American public schools took part in the project: East Oakland School of the Arts in Oakland, California, and Washington High School in Fremont, California—one urban and the other suburban. The third institution involved was a learning center for the poor in a slum of Bangalore, India. Teachers Todd and Ariel from California and Arzu from Bangalore designed the project to raise students' awareness about global living conditions. The project encouraged students to think of themselves as contemporary artists taking part in a global conversation about how the majority of the world population lives. "How do the products you make as an artist relate to your responsibilities as a citizen of the world?" teachers asked.

The unit capitalized on the cultural, socioeconomic, and environmental diversity of the three schools, inviting students to seek to understand one another and respond to one another's work through shared blog and Skype conversations. The unit culminated with the creation of site-specific shelters. For students in the United States, the shelters represented explorations in contemporary art. For students in Bangalore, the project turned into designs for a mobile classroom of the future—a temporary student learning space fit for meditation and study. In their designs, students were inspired to use recycled materials like colorful plastic bags and bottles to filter sunlight, creating a visually rich space for well-being. These students demonstrate global competence learning in the following ways.

Recognizing and expressing their own perspective and identifying the influences on that perspective. For the U.S. students, the project raised awareness of global housing inequality and their own relatively privileged lifestyles. This was especially true for suburban students, who began to look on their own homes with gratitude and a critical eye. Students appreciated their access to technology, not having to earn a living, and the relatively safe and tidy neighborhoods they live in. They came to understand how living in this context influences their perception of standards of living. As one student commented,

> A surprisingly high number of people [around the world] live in shantytowns [and the like] and in poverty. It's funny how people tend to think that everyone lives the same way that they do, probably because we are surrounded by people with the same lifestyles. But when you get out of your comfort zone and really see what is going on, it's crazy. We are so lucky to have what we have.

These students were also able to raise awareness as contemporary artists. As one student noted, "The shelters could create a new light around what a shelter actually is. It's not just a box."

Examining perspectives of other people, groups, or schools of thought. Exchanging images and interacting online enabled students to see one another's environments and analyze differences in culture, styles, and knowledge. Todd's students at Washington High immediately noticed the learning space used by Arzu's students in Bangalore—there, children worked typically on the ground, barefoot, and outdoors. The Indian students' familiarity with natural elements and their awareness of their environment became evident as they offered feedback on Todd's students' designs. The U.S. students recognized that living and learning closer to their natural environment influenced their Indian peers' viewpoints and priorities. Consider the following suggestions from two of Arzu's students:

> Shravya: Have you thought about using your sloped roofs for rainwater collection? The edge of the roofs can have gutters on them. Look at our meditation rooms.
>
> Murali: Are your homes going to have gardens? When we designed our spaces, we had to consider five questions:
>
> 1. How does your space interact with the sun, wind, rain, and acoustics?
>
> 2. How do the physical aspects of the classroom inspire learning (windows, doors, boards, benches, and so on)?
>
> 3. How does your space deal with waste?
>
> 4. How does your space improve the environment/have a positive eco-footprint (food, forests, landscaping, waste, electricity, and so on)?
>
> 5. How does your classroom inspire creative play?

Do these five questions work for your space/models even though they're not a house or classroom?

Explaining how cultural interactions influence and shape perspectives, including the development of ideas. The collaborative nature of this project enabled students from diverse backgrounds to share ideas, influence one another's designs, and recognize similarities in approaches. Shared tasks were potent platforms for collaboration, cross-cultural analysis, and deeper understanding. One of Todd's students commented on sharing techniques for brainstorming:

> I think their poster is visually more appealing than the one we did. It's cool to see people using the same train-of-thought method in a different part of the world. Even though I may not be able to understand what is written on the paper, the technique is relatively similar, and I think that is really neat.

Recognizing inequities in people's experiences and how differences in opportunities and vulnerabilities shape life and perspectives—those of others and their own. Despite their drastically different socioeconomic environments, students in California and Bangalore engaged in a serious reflection about the ways in which food, shelter, and education affect people's lives. The discussion was not limited to material wealth but addressed the conditions that enable well-being, as well as the individual's responsibility to consider the well-being of others. "This unit was a sneak peek into the emotions of homeless people," commented one of Todd's students, "but this peek is not limited to homeless people—it was a way to experience the emotions of any person who has faced [these kinds of] dilemmas in their lives." As Arzu explains,

> The students were engaged in a global conversation about education for all. In heated conversations, students argued whether we needed to design for 40 children, like in our centers, or for 500 children, like in the government school next door. The children were engaged in conversations around quality, scale, and the need for education. As artists, they were a part of global conversations, keeping their real context

(socioeconomic, cultural, geographic, and environmental) in mind.

Arzu believes that reflecting on the importance of education and life experiences can help students reframe how they view their opportunities. Arzu primarily works with the children of construction workers. Here's how she sees their work in this unit:

> We were making the leap from a field they understood and positioning them at the level of a designer with a global consciousness. They presented their work and received feedback from architects and designers in the city, validating the importance of the work they were doing and pushing them to think beyond their concept of school and classroom. One student has continued to pursue this work and has submitted drawings and models in order to build a one-room schoolhouse in her community. Others have designed elaborate rainwater catchment systems based on research of various rainwater-harvesting models.

As this project illustrates, interaction and serious work can help students develop their beliefs about others living on opposite sides of the planet and in strikingly different socioeconomic conditions. Cross-cultural collaboration encourages them to challenge stereotypes and recognize that diversity of perspectives enriches their work—and their understanding of themselves as producers of work.

Examining Laughter in the United States and Afghanistan

"A cheerful heart is good medicine, but a crushed spirit dries up the bones." This biblical proverb opens a well-crafted expository essay by Arthur, an 8th grader from Explorer West School in Seattle, Washington, on the universal biological benefits of laughter. As he explains, "[Laughter] increases the amount of serotonin in your brain, which makes you relax; it also increases the amount of dopamine in your brain, which changes your behavior, making you a happier person, and it helps you maintain a positive outlook on life."

Arthur addresses the reader directly and colorfully. He argues that a central communicative characteristic of humor is that jokes and comedy are interpreted by the listener, who determines the very outcome of a joke—whether it's funny or not. Context and audience matter greatly in "how jokes work." To elaborate on this point, the essay compares cases of American humor with those of humor in Afghanistan. Arthur argues that American humor is "widely determined by observations made by one or multiple people." And it can easily be self-deprecating, as illustrated by the proverb "It is better to be silent and be thought a fool than to speak and remove all doubt."

Humor in Afghanistan has a different structure and social function. "Bidar is [an Afghan] comedian on whom people rely to help them escape from pain and fear," the essay explains. One of his routines is to impersonate someone who is feared, helping people play with their pain. Bidar's popularity in Afghanistan suggests to Arthur that his kind of humor works in that particular context. People in Afghanistan use comedy to forget aggression and heal from violence. In addition, before local elections, remote villagers use humor to promote themselves.

Arthur concludes the essay with a recommendation. To ensure mental and physical well-being, readers are to follow the Taoist monks' tradition of smiling each day. Further, to create a resilient society, he exhorts readers to remember Charlie Chaplin's words: "To truly laugh you must be able to take your pain and play with it."

Arthur's work demonstrates the capacity to recognize perspectives because it expresses his own and others' perspectives on an issue and identifies the influences on those perspectives. Arthur clearly recognizes that humor operates differently in different cultures, and he considers the perspectives involved. First, he comes to see that what he naturally finds funny—jokes that respond to American norms—is only one of many types of humor across the globe. Although he doesn't examine the source of the American preference for observations and self-deprecation, Arthur illustrates his point by citing classic American humorists such as Mark Twain, Ambrose Bierce, Gary Larson, and Bill Watterson.

Arthur understands that humor in war-torn areas like Afghanistan, which he addresses with utmost respect, operates differently from how it does in other places. There, humor is charged with self-preservation and is often used as a tool in power struggles. General references to fear, violence, and aggression characterize a form of humor that plays a strong social role. What can we learn from examining humor in these two cultures? Arthur's conclusion—urging his readers to smile and find humor in pain—suggests a preliminary attempt to strategically integrate two disparate cultural perspectives.

As in the California-Bangalore shelter project, Arthur's work illustrates his developing capacity to view the world from the perspective of a person other than himself—and to understand the context of his own worldview in the process. In so doing, Arthur and his peers learn to revise social stereotypes often pervasive in their surroundings (e.g., of the passive and disempowered poor Indian youth or an Afghan population unable to find any happiness in the midst of war). They develop intercultural sensitivity to compare perspectives and understand how context shapes those perspectives.

Appreciating Perspectives: The Opportunities, the Challenges

For students preparing for a world shaped by migration, for civic participation, for culturally diverse workplaces, and for further academic study, recognizing diverse perspectives is not an optional skill. It's a fundamental necessity of life in the 21st century. Students work through two fundamental challenges to recognizing those perspectives: they must overcome social stereotypes and develop intercultural understanding.

Social stereotypes are typically unconscious, deeply held beliefs. For instance, students may believe that all people in Africa are destitute or that immigrants arrive in a new country to "use local social services." Simply acquiring general knowledge about world history, economics, cultures, or languages is not enough to dispel stereotypes; students can transform those stereotypes by engaging cognitively and emotionally in situations that challenge them—through personal interaction, case studies, and reflection on intercultural experiences. Likewise, learning about other people's values, beliefs, and choices encourages students to develop intercultural awareness—the capacity to understand and relate to diverse worldviews and interact sensitively and competently across cultural contexts. Instead of students experiencing difference as a threat, successful learning for intercultural sensitivity enables them to integrate old and new values, selecting judiciously from each cultural context.

The basis of equality is understanding and empathy, and teachers can do much to promote understanding by designing lessons that require students to learn from various perspectives. Consider the teacher in a U.S. southern state who wanted his students, most of whom identify as Christian, to gain a better understanding of the Islamic faith. He invited his students to read *Persepolis* (Satrapi, 2003), the graphic memoir of an Iranian girl who grew up under the Shah and lived through the Iranian revolution of 1979 before leaving for Europe. She left her family and gained her independence but eventually returned to Iran, her spiritual homeland, in search of her identity.

To put the story in context, the teacher had students research Iranian history, politics, culture, and Islam before and after the revolution. They watched a documentary from inside Iran and listened to a podcast by an Iranian Christian, which helped them make sense of the main character's journey as she struggles to be a loyal daughter, a woman, an Iranian, and a Muslim.

The teacher wanted his students to understand the difference between how Muslims portray their religion and how non-Muslims portray it. He also wanted them to think about how non-Christians portray Christianity and how that made his students feel. "It was a big win," the teacher said, "to get Christian students to make a connection with Islamic characters and for them to see that faith is faith no matter the religion" (Asia Society & OECD, 2018).

Powerful learning experiences invite students to recalibrate their views by shedding light on the multiplicity of factors (gender, age, class, ethnicity) that make up individual identity and the forces shaping them (cultural, political, economic, historical, environmental). To be successful nurturers of global competence in their students, educators must understand the delicate tensions involved in studying other people's worldviews, reflecting on their own perspectives, and offering students ample practice in doing the same in informed and respectful ways. Figure 4.1 outlines some of the developmental pathways toward perspective taking.

Questions to Ponder

- Consider a few moments in your life in which you came to recognize that a person had a cultural perspective or worldview that was very different from your own. What triggered such recognition? What did you come to understand?

Figure 4.1

Understand and Appreciate the Perspectives and Worldviews of Others: Beginning, Learning, Mastering

	Beginning	Learning	Mastering
Recognizing different perspectives and worldviews	Students have a simplistic view of perspectives: one person/ one perspective. They cannot yet explain the roots of a perspective. The students view context as either irrelevant or as deterministic ("context as destiny"). The students view perspectives (cultural, religious, linguistic) as relatively fixed, bounded, or impermeable markers of a person's identity and worldview. They view an individual's identity predominantly in terms of one category (such as nationality or religion). Students don't consider themselves as having a distinct cultural perspective or worldview and believe instead that what they know is "the norm."	Students can identify different actors and points of view on an issue. They begin to recognize that differences in perspectives or worldviews are rooted in cultural, religious, socioeconomic, regional, and other backgrounds and that they also hold a particular view of the world. Students cannot yet articulate how multiple perspectives relate to one another.	Students can describe and interpret multiple perspectives and worldviews. They understand that perspectives are rooted in cultural, religious, socioeconomic, regional, and other backgrounds, and they understand how someone's geographic and cultural context can shape how that person sees the world. They also understand that an individual's identity is complex (one can be a girl, a daughter, a farmer, and a citizen at the same time). In addition, students can articulate relationships among perspectives, placing the perspectives in a broader encompassing frame. (For example, when they see two classmates from different ethnic groups fighting because of cultural prejudices, they understand that the classmates' relationship reflects broader tensions in today's society.)

(continued)

Figure 4.1—(continued)

Understand and Appreciate the Perspectives and Worldviews of Others: Beginning, Learning, Mastering

	Beginning	Learning	Mastering
Recognizing different perspectives and worldviews— (*continued*)			Students view themselves as holding perspectives and blind spots. They understand that their perspective is informed by their context and experiences and that others may perceive them in ways that may differ from the way they see themselves.
Identifying connections, grasping our shared humanity, and recognizing mutual influences across cultural groups	Students do not yet recognize connections among human beings apart from physical connotations and evident cultural markers. They view actions as not affecting individuals from different cultures or contexts; they believe that those distant or exotic "others" must think and behave differently than they do and that they don't share similar rights or needs.	Students recognize that people from different cultures share most basic human rights and needs (for food, shelter, work, education, happiness). They understand the meaning of these rights or needs and some of the desirable ways in which those needs can be met.	Students appreciate common human rights and needs and reflect on individual, cultural, or contextual differences critically, understanding the obstacles that individuals and societies may confront (economic inequality, unequal power relations, violence, unsustainable conduct) in affirming their rights to diversity and well-being. They also understand that universal human rights leave considerable space for national, regional, cultural particularity and other forms of diversity and that the universality of these rights enables human beings, individually and in groups, to pursue their own visions of the good life as long as their choices are consistent with comparable rights for others.

- Examine the diverse backgrounds that your students bring to class. What can you do to make such variety in perspectives visible and valued? How can you instill a climate of recognition and respect and help students learn about their own perspectives and that of others in your classroom?

- Consider the content you teach. Can you enrich particular topics by considering different cultural, economic, religious, regional, or disciplinary perspectives? How may you redesign instruction to nurture students' ability to recognize and express perspectives?

Dimension 3: Communicating Across Differences

Educating globally competent students involves preparing them to interact with people in a world in which multilingualism, diversity, and a mixing of people and cultures are the norm. Globally competent children and youth learn to communicate and build relationships with people from different cultures, geographies, faiths, ideologies, and other factors. This dimension of global competence addresses students' appreciation for respectful dialogue, in person and online.

These students communicate with others in more than one language and across multiple contexts and are sensitive to the cultural norms, interactive styles, and degrees of formality of intercultural contexts. They have learned to appreciate other languages as windows into and expressions of culture, identity, and perspective. They recognize that even in their own language, people bring their own perspectives, life experiences, and cultural identities to communicating with others. For example, students recognize that different people may interpret an expression differently, according to their frame of reference. These students are also sensitive to the fact that the languages we don't speak can be barriers to building relationships, so they are inclined to seek alternative forms of connection.

Globally competent students have learned to listen to others actively and empathetically, suspending judgment and managing ambiguities in communication. These students have learned to bring an open mind to interactions, demonstrating curiosity and a willingness to engage with others and with their perspectives. Students who know more than one language or who straddle cultures and languages themselves, such as immigrant-origin or First Nations students, are an asset to the monolingual classroom because they bring the capacity to listen empathically and manage ambiguities (Boix Mansilla, 2017; Deardorff, 2020; Heath, 1983; James, 2014; National Assessment of Educational Progress, 2019).

Globally competent students can adapt their forms of communication to both formal and informal contexts to express beliefs, share stories, persuade, or comfort. For example, they recognize that talking with a friend about weekend plans requires a different use of language than preparing a formal letter to a government representative. They use multiple languages and symbol systems flexibly in both oral and written contexts, and they appropriately use gestures, images, music, graphs, numbers, and maps, keeping their audience and their purposes in mind.

Globally competent students see the need to be especially attentive and clear in online communication, where text is the sole medium of expression, misunderstandings are possible, and emotions are difficult to convey. They therefore use targeted strategies. For example, our colleague Carrie James (2014) and others at Project Zero have posited that certain moves can help ensure respectful and civil dialogue online. These include *notice* (students carefully read to identify important points in an online communication); *appreciate* (students value aspects of what they read), *probe* (students press for more details), *ask questions* (students get a better sense of another's perspective), and *snip* (students cut and paste something from the original post to signal careful listening or request clarification). Students are also invited to *connect* with their own experience and *extend* the ideas they heard or read, giving their interlocutors a novel perspective.

Globally competent students have learned to reflect on interpersonal and intercultural communication. They can detect communication conflicts, analyze them, and propose solutions. They are critically aware of how power plays out in human communication and seek to recognize others and be recognized with dignity and respect. They have increasingly sophisticated ideas about how language works, how difficulties in communication come about, and what options are at their disposal in their repertoire. Such meta-communicative skills prepare students to engage in thoughtful cross-cultural interactions, seek culturally and linguistically responsive ways to engage others across differences, and meet the goals of multiple participants in a dialogue marked by respect.

Globally competent students do the following:

- **Recognize and value multiple languages and forms of communication**, understanding them as expressions of culture, perspectives, and identity.

- **Listen actively and empathically, with a curious and open mind**, recognizing that cultural perspectives influence communication norms, meaning making, and relationships.

- **Employ verbal and nonverbal languages** and strategies in ways that are appropriate and respectful, given their audience and contexts.

- **Reflect about communication** and the challenges and opportunities it presents to bridge differences, understand self and others, and collaborate in an interdependent world.

How Students Are Communicating Across Differences

Let's now look at two examples of this dimension in action. The first one involves an effort to repurpose school grounds to grow food for a local shelter in Seattle, Washington; the second showcases a project to explore tensions in colonization through contemporary art at the International School of Amsterdam.

Growing Food for the Community

Eighth grade students at the Aki Kurose Middle School in Seattle, Washington, have been studying the effect of global food crises on communities around the world, including their own. Through the Bridges to Understanding after-school program, students analyzed digital stories written by children in India and South Africa, exchanging ideas about rising food prices and community work. Determined to address this global problem by contributing locally, students created two edible gardens at their school. They donated vegetables to the local food bank and produced their own digital story to share.

The digital story and the accompanying discussion forum had two purposes. First, students sought to show how communities can use school fields to mitigate the global food crisis locally. Second, they wanted to gather insights from more experienced gardeners online. The students used both photographs and text to describe the garden design and document its development. Here are two excerpts from their story:

> We started by planting a cover crop in the beds. A cover crop improves and protects the soil on which it is grown. We planted clover and rye in October. These helped improve the quality of the soil during the winter.

> We can use the Native American technique of planting the "three sisters," which are beans, corn, and squash, to benefit the food bank in our community.

Student postings were written in both English and Spanish to accommodate speakers of both languages.

These students demonstrated their capacity to engage in open, appropriate, and effective interactions by doing the following.

Listening actively and empathically, recognizing how diverse audiences may perceive different meanings from the same information. Students explored the complexity of communicating with diverse audiences by first examining the diversity in their own classrooms. In a school where multiple languages are spoken at home, students created cultural self-portraits that revealed their unique perspectives. Appreciating difference within the classroom set the foundation to embrace it globally online. How might others interpret the humorous note at the end of one online posting? How might others feel about our story and our relatively protected world?

A teacher in rural India who participated in the forum expressed his appreciation in learning about food banks for the first time. Describing himself as a farmer, he inquired whether there were many farmers in the school. Students seized the opportunity to explain how food banks work and clarify their role as "gardeners":

> A food bank is a community resource for people who don't have enough money or food to support their family. We will feel accomplishment when we harvest the food.

> We have two raised garden beds behind our school. We don't consider ourselves farmers…we are gardeners who do this for fun and for the community.

Employing verbal and nonverbal languages and strategies appropriately and respectfully, given the audience and contexts. Students' postings show an understanding of online etiquette and communicative norms, as well as a growing capacity to communicate effectively with diverse people. Their writing is informal and engaging, and each entry closes with a question inviting readers to participate. The following is an example of one student's post:

> We have made a digital story for all of you to see! It's about us growing crops at our school for the food bank. Do any of you have gardens at your schools? If so, what are you growing? What happens to the food you grow?
>
> If you don't have a school garden, do you grow food at home? Where do you get your food? Do you have any special techniques for planting or gardening? We learned about "the three sisters"—squash, corn, and beans—which we might plant this spring. :) Talk to you soon!

Aware of their international audience, students agreed not to use common American text messaging norms, understanding that English may be the third or fourth language of their readers. Extensive use of symbols and shorthand would make their communication ineffective.

Digital storytelling requires that students simultaneously manage visual, auditory, and textual material. For example, to convey the message as powerfully as possible, the choice of photographs to include depends on such concepts as composition and lighting and how well the images express emotion and movement. The accompanying text, offered in both English and Spanish, follows a similar selection process. In the end, students' close attention to communicative choices enabled them to participate proficiently in an international conversation—and learn with and about others in the process.

Exposing the Plight of the Colonized:
"Put Your Culture in That Box, and Follow Me!"

For the final project of their contemporary music, art, and theater class, 10th graders at the International School of Amsterdam had to create a "happening"—a fleeting artistic event or installation in the school. Their task was to explore the concept of exile in aesthetically interesting and novel ways. A happening conducted by Mary, Maiko, Paul, and Yan examined colonization as a metaphor for forced exile. The group chose to include the audience (teachers, researchers, and special invitees) because they "wanted the audience to really get a sense of what colonization might feel like." They dressed in black, faces half covered by masks, and yelled commands simultaneously at their audience in their four different native languages. Participants were unable to understand what the students said, but strong gestures indicated they were to follow the students through various stations in the happening.

The students wanted to elicit from their audience a sense of powerlessness and frustration to make them feel as though they really were being "colonized." As pressure for obedience mounted, all attempts at two-way communication broke down, and the captive audience began to quietly follow the masked students. Participants were instructed to place their shawls, watches, and shoes in a box marked "Pre-Colonial History Museum"; they were then forced to carry labels with their newly modified names.

These students demonstrated their capacity to engage in open, appropriate, and effective interactions by doing the following.

Recognizing and valuing multiple forms of communication, and understanding them as expressions of culture, perspectives, and identity. The students' happening demonstrated a sophisticated understanding of how the colonized and their colonizers interpret differently their realities, behavior, and artifacts. The symbolic act of relinquishing personally meaningful everyday objects to a "museum" is just one effective strategy the students used to convey such a clash of interpretations.

Employing verbal and nonverbal languages and strategies appropriately, given the audience, context, and purpose. The students integrated a range of artistic modes of expression to convey their message. As they noted, "We chose masks to symbolize the difference in cultures. Once we put our masks on, we were not really ourselves anymore." Using a cacophony of voices and urgent, authoritarian gestures, they communicate with an audience used to very different forms of input. The students related their work to that of other contemporary artists, such as John Cage, who expanded musical expression, and Kara Walker, whose visual work examines the perverse nature of "paternalistic oppression."

Reflecting on communication and on the challenges and opportunities it presents to bridge differences, understand self and others, and collaborate in an interdependent world. The students' work offers a critique of ethnocentrism, the inability to listen, the absence of respect, and other barriers to cross-cultural cooperation. Hailing from different cultural backgrounds, these students comment on and exploit their own linguistic diversity to advance a common aesthetic goal. By engaging in a rich examination of communication—its limits, pitfalls, and potential for abuse—students raise awareness of the responsibilities associated with verbal and nonverbal expression in communicating with others, near or far.

Communicating Across Differences: The Opportunities, the Challenges

Teaching students to communicate competently across cultural, socioeconomic, religious, and personal differences requires that instructors create multiple opportunities for students to practice and reflect on complex communication. This requires a high level of sophistication. In the United States, the Common Core State Standards (2009) highlight the importance of this skill. Writing is seen as

> a key means to assert and defend claims, showing what [students] know and conveying what they have experienced, imagined, thought, and felt…taking task, purpose, and audience into careful consideration and choosing world information structures and formats deliberately.

Beyond language, disciplines such as mathematics, the arts, history, geography, dance, science, and health provide important tools (linguistic, graphic, gestural, technological) to persuade, debate, contest, narrate, describe, and build consensus among individuals who experience the world in different ways. Reflective communication activities like the two examples we have described help students to not only understand the context of communication (communicators' perspectives, intentionality, constraints), but also develop communicative sensitivity.

Expressions that seem rather transparent and self-evident to one person, for example, may prove ambiguous or obscure to another who may interpret them with a different frame of mind. Likewise, comparisons across languages and contexts may help students understand that people in different cultures communicate differently, not simply because they use different words, but also because they share different norms. For instance, a student may come to appreciate that people have different levels of comfort with disagreement, that turn taking in a conversation works in a different way in another context, or that sharing emotions and experiences is more or less common in different social groups. These students are able to "translate" communication styles and adapt their behavior to become more effective communicators. Most important, they don't assess others' communicative styles against the standards of their own cultural patterns. Rather, they bring a pluralistic and respectful attitude to their interactions, recognizing difference as a matter of fact.

In their work with teachers, both Asia Society and UNESCO have adopted a protocol developed by Darla Deardorff of Duke University to promote cross-cultural understanding among students, which she has used in schools worldwide. The *story circles process* (Deardorff, 2020) builds on students' reflections on the first time they became aware of differences among people based on skin color, dress, language, religion, or other distinguishing characteristics. After the students have each told their story, each one briefly says what he or she found most memorable about the stories. The teacher then asks a series of probing questions: What themes did the stories have in common? What surprised us? How will the stories affect your interactions in the future with people from different backgrounds? Afterward, the whole group debriefs, and students write a reflection on how their views have changed. Deardorff says that wherever in the world she's used the protocol, she has seen profound changes in students' views of their fellow students after just a single story-circle session—for instance, students were more empathetic and able to understand the complexities of identity and life in a grounded way (Asia Society & OECD, 2018).

Mapping progressions in students' capacity to communicate across differences can help educators clarify their goals and aspirations for students and guide their feedback and instructional designs. Figure 5.1 offers a helpful progression snapshot.

Figure 5.1

Engage in Open, Appropriate, and Effective Interactions Across Cultures and Differences: Beginning, Learning, Mastering

Beginning	Learning	Mastering
Students don't yet understand how to be effective and appropriate in their communication and that communication must be responsive to audience and context. Specifically, they don't recognize cultural norms, interactive styles, expectations, or levels of formality of a given social and cultural context and audience. Students are not yet able to observe, listen actively, and interpret social and contextual clues, such as body language, tone, diction, physical interactions, dress code, or silences. They are surprised by any breakdowns in communication and lack a communicative repertoire to resolve or prevent those breakdowns.	Students are aware of their way of communicating and attempt to make that communication fit the context. Students can identify some interactive styles, expectations, or levels of formality in a given social and cultural context, but they cannot yet calibrate their language and communication choices accordingly. Students can respond to breakdowns in communication (e.g., by requesting repetitions or reformulations), even if still tentatively.	Students are aware of their own styles of communication and understand how, to be effective and appropriate, they must adapt communication to audience, purpose, and context. Specifically, they are sensitive to nuances in cultural norms, interactive styles, expectations, and levels of formality of a given social and cultural context and audience. They listen actively, observe carefully, and gather insights, including social and cultural clues that inform their communicative choices. Students can manage breakdowns in communication, providing restatements, revisions, or simplifications of their own communication. They employ linguistic devices, such as avoiding categorical claims, connecting to what others said, sharing questions and puzzles, and acknowledging contributions in ways that advance civil and reciprocal dialogue.

Source: From *Preparing Our Youth for an Inclusive and Sustainable World: The OECD PISA Global Competence Framework* (p. 29), 2018, OECD. Copyright 2018 by OECD.

Questions to Ponder

- Consider individuals you know. Can you identify a few who model the capacity to communicate with diverse audiences? What do they do to be effective? In your view, how valuable is this capacity?

- Pay close attention to the forms of communication that are typically used in your classroom. Do you use multiple media? Are statements typically categorical and definitive, or do they show curiosity and invite productive dialogue?

- Consider the content you teach. Do particular topics lend themselves to communication with diverse audiences? How may reflecting on communication enrich students' understanding of the topics under study?

Dimension 4: Taking Action

Globally competent students do more than acquire knowledge about the world: They seek to make a difference. They don't postpone their contributions for "when I grow up" (Allen, 2016, 2019; Allen & Light, 2015; Fischman et al., 2004; James, 2014; Kahne et al., 2015; Parham & Allen, 2015). Instead, they create opportunities to act today in their immediate environments of family and school, in their neighborhoods, or on the global stage. Alone or in collaboration, they weigh options for action on the basis of evidence and insight. They can assess the effect of their plans, taking into account varied perspectives and potential consequences for others. And they demonstrate courage in acting and in reflecting on those actions.

This dimension of global competence highlights young people's role as active and responsible members of society. In a world rife with rapid changes, environmental vulnerabilities, and racial inequities, young people have already demonstrated their collective commitment to a better world. An education for global competence supports and encourages students to express their voice and exercise their influence in thoughtful and informed ways.

Globally competent students are able to take action by doing the following:

- **Identifying and creating opportunities for personal or collaborative action** to address situations, events, issues, or phenomena in ways that improve conditions.

- **Assessing options and planning actions** on the basis of evidence and the potential for impact, taking into account previous approaches, varied perspectives, and potential consequences.

- **Acting personally or collaboratively in creative and ethical ways** to contribute to improvement locally, regionally, or globally and assessing the effect of the actions taken.

- **Reflecting on their capacity to advocate for and contribute to improvement** locally, regionally, or globally toward more inclusive, just, and sustainable societies.

How Students Are Taking Action

The three examples of student work that follow examine the challenges and opportunities students encounter when taking action. The first is an essay by a 4th grader in Britain about the children of political refugees, which received a young journalist award. The second features the work of 9th graders in Buenos Aires, Argentina, who seek to preserve pre-Columbian musical traditions put at risk by globalization. And the third showcases the work of public high school seniors in San Antonio, Texas, who argue for an immediate solution to the water contamination crisis in Thailand.

Raising Awareness About Children in Detention Centers

Lydia, a student at Drayton Park Primary School in London, is 11 years old. She has a strong interest in World War II, triggered by the books of such writers as Morris Gleitzman and Michael Morpurgo, as well as by the diary of Anne Frank. When she learned about a competition run by Amnesty International and *The Guardian* newspaper calling for a report on human rights, she remembered a conversation she recently had at home. Lydia and her parents were talking about human rights, and the conversation turned to the topic of detention centers in the United Kingdom. A study had recently shown the harmful and long-lasting psychological and physical effects on the children of refugees forced into detention centers.

Prompted by her desire to raise awareness about the issue, Lydia began conducting her own research. Her findings are captured in her essay, "Is This Nazi Germany?", which won the upper primary category of Amnesty International's Young Human Rights Reporter of the Year 2010 Award. Written more than a decade ago, Lydia's essay has proven relevant. Migration, both voluntary and involuntary, has increased exponentially since then, and so have detention centers that are now so present in the media. Here is an excerpt from her essay:

> She wakes, as eight men in dark uniforms barge through her front door. Her mother screams, but she stays riveted to the spot, shaking uncontrollably. The men hand her mother some paper and ignore her screams of outrage.
>
> The men search the house. It is turned upside down. Abruptly, they are both frogmarched to the back of a van. They don't know where they are going or how long they will remain in this dark, enclosed space.
>
> This is not Nazi Germany; this is September 2009 in Leeds [England]. Bethlehem Abate is 11 years old and has escaped with her mother from Ethiopia, where she was abused by her father. If she returns to Ethiopia, she will be separated from her mother, who is Eritrean. She will have no one to care for her. Her mother will be put in detention or even be killed by the authorities.
>
> Yarl's Wood is situated in Bedfordshire; it is a detention center for asylum seekers. Each year, there is an intake of 1,000 children. It is not a place for children. No child should be deprived of their education and freedom in this way.
>
> As Bethlehem entered Yarl's Wood, she said, "It was like going into prison, for doing an awful crime. I thought the British government would understand our situation and help us."
>
> Bethlehem and her mother have now been granted the right to remain in this country. They look back at their time in Yarl's Wood with horror. Many others are not so fortunate.

This student's essay demonstrates her capacity to take action by the following.

Identifying and creating opportunities for action to address situa-tions in ways that improve conditions. Reading about children's experi-ences in detention centers disturbed Lydia. Encouraged by her parents and teachers, Lydia decided the essay contest was a good opportunity to write about the topic. She explains,

> Before we talked about it, I had no idea that human rights violations were happening in England. I always thought that human rights violations were things that happened in India or Africa, and I had no idea they were happening here. It was horrible.

In her view, the essay would help "raise awareness about children in detention centers. No child should suffer this appalling lack of education and lack of freedom." Lydia decided that focusing on a girl of about her age would be an effective narrative technique, highlighting the contrast between her own safe and comfortable life and the very different life of her subject. Lydia's essay seeks to build on the tradition of girls from the past she admires, like Anne Frank.

Acting collaboratively in creative and ethical ways to contribute to improvement. Getting recognition for her essay led Lydia to think about doing even more for refugee children. She joined a young cam-paigners' group at Amnesty International that worked to increase public awareness in the United Kingdom, where the government is deciding to abolish child detention, granting children of refugees legal status on arrival. Lydia adds,

> I am really hoping that I can make a difference. Many cam-paigners are working to make detention centers better. I understand that we may have to have detention centers, but you don't have to call them such horrible names, you don't have to torture people there—not physical torture, but psy-chological torture. You don't have to put them through such a horrible and very destructive experience that has a big impact on people's lives…, leaving them scarred for life.

Reflecting on her capacity to advocate for and contribute to more inclusive, just, and sustainable societies. Asked whether she, as a child, can make a difference, Lydia replies with hope that she can contribute to the work that many others are doing. Grateful for all the support she has received, she understands the key role played by her family and those teachers who encouraged her to voice her opinion. She enjoys the feeling of having found a cause that matters to her—abolishing child detention centers and knowing that "whatever happens, you stood up for something you believed in."

Promoting the Survival of Andean Musical Heritage

Sara, a 9th grader in St. George School in Buenos Aires, Argentina, was puzzled over her music teacher's assertion that globalization is increasing the homogenization of music and, as a result, that traditional pre-Columbian rhythms, cultures, and artifacts from the Andes region are disappearing. To address this problem, Sara's class conducted an in-depth study of Andean musical, artistic, and cultural heritage. After weighing options, the class decided to create a sustainable initiative to promote the survival of pre-Columbian artifacts and music, which Sara documents in her final report.

The class built a series of *sikus* (traditional Andean flutes) with recycled materials. Carefully designed to produce tones on a pentatonic scale, the sikus were made of recycled paper and illustrated with carefully selected and stylized traditional Andean art motifs. To help preserve this cultural tradition, Sara's class proceeded to teach the migrant children in a poor neighborhood school how to produce, decorate, and play sustainable sikus themselves. Proud of her class's accomplishment, Sara comments that among the kids in the barrio, "autochthonous music is more socially accepted as a form of cultural expression." She concludes her report with a hopeful observation: projects like the one her class conducted involve "a new phase in a process that goes from discrimination, racism, and intolerance to acceptance, admiration, respect, and inclusion of all inhabitants in our cities, [as well as] their practices and cultural expressions."

Sara and her peers demonstrate their capacity to take action by doing the following.

Identifying and creating opportunities to address an issue in ways that advance more inclusive, just, and sustainable societies and assessing options and planning actions on the basis of evidence and the potential for impact. Sara's global competence begins with her genuine concern about the loss of her cultural heritage in the face of globalization. Excitement about the opportunity to contribute keeps her engaged throughout the project: she knows she can make a difference. In tackling the problem, Sara, her teachers, and her peers considered several possible courses of action, such as organizing a school concert or writing an article for the school newspaper. They finally decided that a multiweek interdisciplinary unit on art history and sustainable instrument design promised the longest-lasting effect, especially if they could share their work with children whose families were direct descendants of Andean populations.

Acting collaboratively, in creative and ethical ways, to contribute to improvement and reflecting on their capacity to act. Developing functional sikus required the participation of most students in the class. Some students tested and budgeted materials, some led the collection of recycled paper, others prepared to perform for the barrio children, and still others researched traditional melodies to play. Students demonstrate global competence and the capacity to act when they organize multiple actors around a common goal. Sara's report reflects on the class's success in creating working sikus (itself not a minor challenge) and learning how to play the instrument. Finally, she notes in her reflections that working with children proved to be the most challenging aspect of the project:

> Standing in front of children who were almost my age and who did not seem interested in the project in the beginning was difficult. Fortunately, the children changed their attitude in the process. I was able to meet with a few and teach them how to make sikus so they would keep the music alive. I am confident that the children were engaged and planned to create sikus of their own. We even left the materials for them to work with. Now whether or not our project overall will be successful, only time will tell.

Seeking Solutions to a Water Pollution Crisis

In the International School of the Americas, in San Antonio, Texas, students in Emma's macroeconomics class are presenting their development proposals to a panel of teachers, school administrators, and students. Their teacher had set the challenge a few weeks before:

> The World Bank is giving the United Nations extra money to help to increase the effectiveness of the Millennium Development Goals. Your group is a part of a nongovernmental organization that hopes to receive a subsidy to implement a project that would help to stimulate economic growth by targeting a particular problem evident in a developing country. Create a proposal that would demonstrate why your organization's project would create economic growth in a particular country. Explain the gravity of the problem and the effects your development project would have on this country using at least two economic models.

Five students chose to seek solutions to the water pollution crisis in Thailand. As they note,

> One third of the [available fresh] water is unsuitable for human consumption. High levels of water pollution exist in many rivers, lakes, and the surrounding ocean. Heavy metals such as arsenic and lead [are commonly found] in the water. Drought vulnerability is high in the Northeast. More than 100,000 [annual] hospitalizations are due to waterborne diseases, and only 29 percent of the population can be supported by the current quantity of filtered water.

To contextualize the problem, they share basic indicators of the country's economic development (e.g., gross domestic product [GDP] per capita, urbanization, unemployment, literacy) and describe seasonal changes to water availability in various regions. They share a brief economic history of the country and describe Thai culture as one of Buddhism-inspired "forgive and forget."

The students' proposal is aimed at "providing reliable infrastructure to store, filter, and distribute potable water to the 7,000 people in the area, as well as educating citizens about the importance of clean water and how to access it." They designed their intervention for Ban Lao Kwang, in the Phitsanulok province, at a total cost of $1.5 million. Their presentation includes a detailed budget and an outline of the expected effect of the project, not only on water availability, but also on economic growth. In the short term, they expect an improvement in local unemployment and a slight increase in GDP due to an increase in demand of materials. In the long term, they predict increases in agricultural productivity and human development indicators. They also expect educated people from the surrounding areas to improve water conditions. Figure 6.1 shows two economic models they used for their predictions.

Figure 6.1
Water Pollution in Thailand: Two Economic Models

Increase Demand and Increase Supply

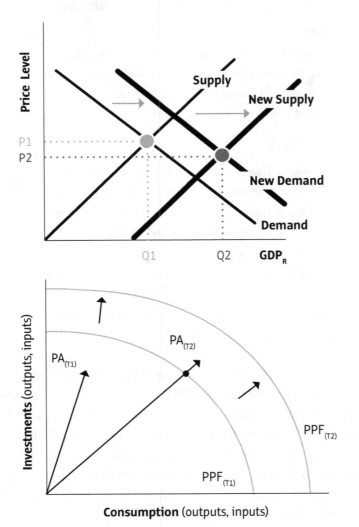

This work demonstrates their capacity to take action in the following ways.

- **Assessing options and planning actions on the basis of evidence and potential impact.** The assignment created a sense of urgency in students; they had to identify a problem worth addressing. Drawing from their detailed study of the region, their understanding of development options, and their knowledge of macroeconomics, the students were able to suggest solutions and predict implications. Their solutions were directly informed by a review of other water-related initiatives led by Oxfam, Water First, and UNICEF, whom they propose as funders of their project.

The project has proven to be of long-lasting benefit to the students and to their sense of themselves as agents of change. The following spring, during a visit to the World Bank in Washington, D.C., they shared their ideas with experts and asked questions about the bank's Millennium Development Goal strategies. Their teacher describes the visit as follows:

> The visit to the World Bank [showed that] students retained the information they learned and were intently passionate about learning more in the area of international development. They quickly responded to questions [by the bank's representatives] about strategies to stimulate development in various countries. The presenter was impressed with the knowledge my students had over international development and their ideas on the pathways to help achieve the Millennium Development Goals.

Students felt that this visit to the bank was the most significant experience they had during that trip because it enabled them to see how they could apply their skills toward positive change. Several students indicated that they would like to do an internship at the bank during their college years. The opportunity to create and assess solutions to a pressing humanitarian problem meant much more to these students than simply completing a school task. It prompted them to begin viewing themselves as global citizens.

Taking Action: The Opportunities, the Challenges

Taking action on matters of local, global, and intercultural significance enriches the scholastic orientation of schools by incorporating a range of authentic real-world experiences. It capitalizes on youth's desire to participate and make a difference on issues and for people they care about. Students begin to see that they can be vocal participants in world events. They can voice informed views and influence opinions and actions. By taking action on matters of local, global, and intercultural significance, students learn to overcome cultural biases, build relationships with allies, and view themselves as "present"—not just "future"—citizens.

Yet participation is not always easy. Research suggests that young people who are willing to state their positions publicly—and especially digitally—often receive backlash (Allen & Light, 2015). To prepare them for equitable, effective, and self-protective civic participation, our colleague Danielle Allen and her team propose that young people keep a series of considerations in mind. They need to consider which aspects of their identity they should share publicly, given current and future audiences. As students take their idea from "I" to "we," they need to decide what kind of supports they will need along the way. They will also have to anticipate backlash and decide in advance how to strategize around it. And they will need to find allies who can sustain and empower their work.

Let's look at one more example of how taking action can connect students' learning to issues of social justice, leading to real change in a community. Andrea Ramirez Garcia teaches a class called "Mexico and the Global Agenda" at a private secondary school outside Mexico City (Asia Society & OECD, 2018). She wanted her students to learn through experience about the rule of law, what it means to be an active citizen in a democracy, and the concept of social justice. She also wanted them to realize that they could make a difference in their community.

As part of a unit to teach students how to evaluate a political, a social, or an economic challenge and come up with a solution, Garcia had students create and administer to the public a survey about their attitudes and experiences with corruption. They learned that about 75 percent of the people had been victims of corruption but that many did not even recognize it because it was so commonplace. The students also found that many of those who *did* realize that corruption was in play and that it was wrong had done nothing about it, either because they felt powerless or because they didn't know how to register a complaint or seek a resolution.

Her students then came up with a plan for how to reduce corruption and presented it to local elected officials. Garcia says, "They don't usually get to have a voice, everything they learn is hypothetical, so when they're actually doing things and their voices are heard, they feel what it's like to make a difference, and they feel empowered" (Asia Society & OECD, 2018).

Figure 6.2 offers a schema for teachers to think about progressions in students' capacity for informed and ethical action in local, global, and intercultural environments.

Questions to Ponder

- Consider your own concentric spheres of action—family, community, nation, globe. What specific actions could you take to improve conditions in each sphere?

- How competent are your students in social entrepreneurship and collaborative project design? What do they need to learn to be ready for college, work, and the world?

- Consider the content you teach. Do particular topics lend themselves naturally to creating opportunities for global action?

Figure 6.2

Take Action for Collective Well-Being and Sustainable Development: Beginning, Learning, Mastering

	Beginning	Learning	Mastering
Evaluating actions	Students consider one course of action as obvious and unproblematic. For example, when they're presented with a problem about industrial pollution, their immediate conclusion would be to "just close all polluting factories."	Students understand that multiple courses of action are possible to address an issue/situation or contribute to the well-being of individuals and societies. They can identify directions for future investigations if the available evidence is insufficient for reaching conclusions about the best course of action.	Students can identify and evaluate different courses of action to solve an issue/situation. They weigh these actions against one another by looking at precedents, considering and evaluating available evidence, and assessing the conditions that may make actions possible.
Assessing consequences	Students understand the implications that follow from simple actions in linear terms without weighing multiple actions and implications or considering unintended consequences.	Students understand the most likely immediate consequences of a given position or course of action and can assess how these consequences compare with those following alternative positions/views.	Students consider the immediate and indirect consequences or implications of different possible actions and decisions. They can weigh short- and long-term consequences, as well as short-range and spatially distant consequences. They also consider the possibility of unintended consequences of actions.

Source: From *Preparing Our Youth for an Inclusive and Sustainable World: The OECD PISA Global Competence Framework* (p. 29), 2018, OECD. Copyright 2018 by OECD.

Teaching for Global Competence

Over the last decades, researchers and practitioners have identified key capacities teachers need to develop to teach for global competence with quality. Among them are the disposition for "empathy and for valuing multiple perspectives" and "a commitment to equity." Our own work at Project Zero has highlighted the centrality of teachers' curiosity, as well as their formal and experiential understanding of the world. For example, teachers who grew up in bicultural contexts or who traveled or studied abroad were likely to draw on these personal experiences as a source of self-efficacy in their efforts to teach about local and global issues. Bilingual teachers viewed themselves as especially ready to invite students to learn new languages and understand new cultures (Crawford et al., 2020; Tichnor-Wagner et al., 2019). The teachers valued their growing capacity to facilitate difficult conversations regarding complex global issues and design classrooms that would be responsive to their students' cultural backgrounds, experiences, and assets—classrooms that embody a culture of global competence.

In fact, the more familiar teachers become with high-quality teaching for global competence, the clearer it is that this kind of teaching is not an add-on, but rather a shift in the way we teach the topics in our courses. They also see that educating for global competence takes place through direct instruction—by creating learning environments where understanding the world and acting on that understanding are part of the values, expectations, rituals, interactions, and language that constitute the culture of a classroom or a school.

So just what does quality teaching for global competence look like? The short answer is that it's *varied*. Projects or units may vary in scope (short extensions of a unit or whole-school projects); they vary in the types of disciplines involved (e.g., art, math, languages, literature, history, economics); they vary in the levels of education involved (preschool to graduate school); and they vary depending on the geopolitical perspective they embody (liberal to conservative). Yet across these variations, four questions should rest front and center while designing instruction for global competence (Boix Mansilla & Schleicher, 2022):

- What topics matter most to teach?
- What will students take away from a unit, project, visit, or course?
- What will students do to learn?
- How will we know if students are making progress?

Our colleague David Perkins (1992), a cognition and instruction expert at Project Zero, calls these "Pandora questions." Simple on the surface, they can lead to intricate and fascinating reflection once we seek to answer them.

In a nutshell, this chapter proposes that high-quality instruction for global competence requires teachers to

- Identify engaging topics of local and global significance.
- Focus on global competence outcomes.
- Design performances of global competence.
- Employ ongoing global competence-centered assessment.

Teaching for Global Competence: An Earth Science Example

Let's begin by looking at an example of teaching for global competence. Rosa Lin teaches 9th grade Earth System and Planetary Sciences at Wellesley High School, a public school in Massachusetts. Here's how she describes her course:

> Earth science is *awesome!* Earth scientists love discovering,
> being curious, exploring, and enjoying the challenge (and
> process) of figuring things (the earth) out. You need a good
> imagination, too, because you have to imagine where the
> clues might be, then find the clues, and then figure out what
> the clues mean.
>
> We use our "knowns" to confront the "unknowns" through
> investigations and a science way of thinking. Sometimes we
> have to revise our so-called "knowns" because we didn't get
> it right, or we had it only partially right, or we missed some-
> thing, but the goal in science is always a deeper understand-
> ing…. Our planet is a dynamic, ever-changing place. We will
> try to fathom the forces at work on earth so we can better
> understand, appreciate, and care for our planet, our fellow
> living things, and the planetary systems that sustain life.

In this course, students learn to think of the earth both as a body
in dynamic interaction with other bodies in the universe and as a system in which various forces are in dynamic interaction. They examine,
for instance, the constant circulation of water through the earth's
hydrosphere, geosphere, biosphere, and atmosphere. Students are
expected to understand how the water cycle works and interacts with
biogeochemical cycles such as carbon, oxygen, and nitrogen to produce
changes in the earth's planetary system.

The course's final unit invites students to apply their understanding
of the earth system to the complex phenomenon of climate change.
Students learn about the past causes of climate change, the available
evidence, the changes observed today, the driving forces, the time
frames, and future projections. They consider such questions as these:
What makes the earth switch from a hot house to an ice age? Over what
period of time does such a change occur? How are changes today similar
to and different from changes in the past? How may we mitigate global
warming?

The four Pandora questions offer a good framework for considering
how to teach global competence (see Figure 7.1).

Let's now look at each Pandora question in more depth.

Figure 7.1
Teaching for Global Competence: Four Pandora Questions

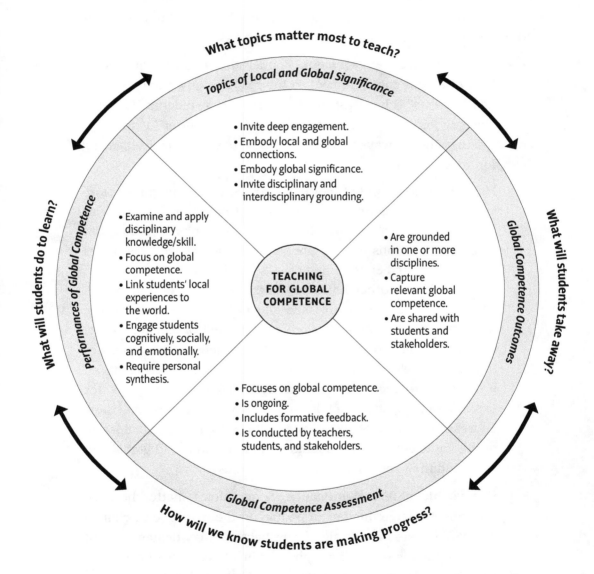

What Topics Matter Most to Teach?

Defining the topics that students should learn in a course or project can be challenging. There's so much to learn about the world today, and constraints on time and resources make decisions about what to teach ever more crucial and challenging. Four criteria are essential here:

- **Generates deep engagement.** Ponder the following questions: How does this topic connect to the reality of my students' lives and interests? How might this topic appear in students' lives outside school? Am I passionate about the topic myself? If so, why? Are there better ways to frame this topic to make it truly engaging for my students?

- **Has clear local-global connections.** Students might explore cultural variations on themes common to all humanity, such as language, motherhood, or friendship. Other units may consider global explanations of local phenomena, such as why gas prices rise in the United States when there's a political crisis in the Middle East. In still other units, teachers may focus on differences and similarities in how an issue affects two or more locations; for example, students might look at the effect of climate change on coastal and noncoastal cities. Or students might consider the effect of global policy, such as international agreements to protect environments, on local issues. When framing a topic for exploration, consider the following: In what ways does this topic address local and global dynamics? How may a deep examination of this topic enable my students to understand broad global patterns and their relationship to local realities?

- **Has visible global significance.** Some topics matter because they affect a large number of people on the planet (e.g., climate change). Others may be significant because they demand urgent global solutions (e.g., girls' right to education, global health and security) or because they directly affect students' lives (e.g., migration in local neighborhoods).

- **Has robust disciplinary and interdisciplinary grounding.** Disciplinary knowledge and skill are necessary to interpret situations and create solutions. Strong topics are not framed as facts to memorize (e.g., what are the top traditional foods in Mexico? In

Ethiopia?). Rather, they introduce problems and complexities for students to wrestle with (e.g., how do regional landscapes influence food traditions in Mexico and Ethiopia?). A strong topic demands expertise in more than one subject area and requires students to synthesize knowledge from multiple disciplines.

Choosing Powerful Topics in Rosa Lin's Earth Science Class

Here, students apply their understanding of earth systems and planetary change to a problem of global significance—climate change. Students explore a number of questions: How do sun and earth systems interact to drive earth's climate system? What do we know about natural and manmade causes of climate change, past and present? How can we interpret the latest evidence of global climate change and its effects around the planet? What are the major climate-related concerns, unknowns, and opportunities for the future in different regions?

Lin's framing of climate change appeals to students interested in environmental preservation, as well as in cutting-edge science and public debate around the issue. The unit engages students in a problem they deem relevant to their future—one that demands urgent solutions (*deep engagement*). The unit's open-ended questions encourage disciplinary exploration into such realms as chemistry, physics, geology, and astronomy. In addition, students will need to be able to interpret scientific evidence and maintain the kind of healthy skepticism that strengthens scientific claims (*disciplinary grounding*). The topic also invites students to connect global physical and chemical processes to the local effects of climate change. For example, students study the melting of glaciers at high altitudes, which affects the summer water supply in places like Bolivia and California and, possibly, the frequency and intensity of hurricanes in the Atlantic and South Pacific oceans. Students complete the unit with a deep understanding of the earth as an integrated global system with local implications (*local-global connections*). Finally, a scientific understanding of climate change prepares students to make sense of the powerful forces transforming environments and societies alike, such as the effect of water availability on population displacements, expanding tropical disease vectors, and the human cost of extreme weather events (*global significance*).

Effective teachers examine their curricula, looking for opportunities to make meaningful global connections. A history unit may place the

American Revolution in the context of other contemporary developments around the world, shedding light on mutual influences. A unit on habitats may invite students to compare the delicate balance of life at the local pond with other habitats around the world. By incorporating a global dimension into their curricula, teachers can enrich students' understanding of both the world and their local realities.

What Will Students Take Away?

Teachers can promote deep understanding in this area by targeting clear and manageable learning goals that focus on global competences. When crafting learning goals, teachers may ask the following questions: What disciplinary knowledge (concepts, facts, theories) and skills (methods, tools, techniques) will enable my students to make sense of the topic? What global competences matter most to engage this topic in a meaningful way? How can I make the learning goals in this project clear?

Strong learning goals do the following:

- **Capture important knowledge and skills in one or more disciplines.** Teaching for global competence means using curriculum content, usually set forth in learning standards, to examine broader global issues. For example, a unit in economics may seek to help students understand gross domestic product (GDP) and how it is calculated; instructors may ask students to use the concept of GDP to compare economic growth in China and the United States. A unit in biology may focus on photosynthesis and respiration and their role in air purification. Here, students may apply their knowledge of the carbon cycle to explain the role that forests play in mitigating global warming.

- **Focus on relevant global competences.** A project on HIV/AIDS in Mombasa, Kenya, may call on students to *investigate the world* and *recognize perspectives*, whereas a project on digital storytelling may require students to *communicate ideas* with diverse audiences. A grassroots project teaching local children about pre-Columbian cultures can spur students to *take action*. For clarification on which aspects of global competence matter most in a given subject area—in the arts, English language arts, mathematics, science, social studies, and world languages—check out the global competence matrices included in the Appendix (see p. 142).

- **Are clearly shared with students.** Each unit should address only a few key goals, which the teacher must explicitly share with students. Post key learning expectations on classroom walls and include them on assignment sheets and in class reflections. Share them with parents, members of the school community, and other stakeholders supporting student development.

Focusing Learning Goals in Rosa Lin's Earth Science Class

Rosa Lin's course invites students to learn how sciences like biology, chemistry, and physics come together in earth science. The course emphasizes scientific inquiry. To that end, students have sought out scientists' accounts of various phenomena by watching video interviews and interacting with visiting scientists in class, contacting scientists directly, and reading articles in such publications as *Scientific American*, *National Geographic*, *Science News*, and *Astronomy* magazine.

Lin has three major learning goals for her students, which simultaneously meet the state's standards, the school's expectations, and the criteria for quality global competence instruction:

- **Learning goal 1: How the earth's spheres and systems interact to influence the climate.** Key concepts: geosphere; biosphere; atmospheric chemistry; hydrosphere; the water and carbon cycle; surface processes (like weathering); astronomical forces (sun, orbit, and meteor impacts)

- **Learning goal 2: How scientists gather and interpret evidence of changing planetary temperatures past and present and what conclusions they reach.** Key ideas: evidence in areas like biology, chemistry, physics, and paleoclimatology; scientific method; experiments; available data from locations (especially the poles and high-altitude and coastal regions)

- **Learning goal 3: How to evaluate and promote solutions and policies to mitigate climate change.** Key ideas: the impact of alternative energy sources, nuclear energy, green technologies, environmental architecture, carbon sequestration, burial of carbon in ultramafic rock, and creation of fuels from microbes

What Will Students Do to Learn?

In high-quality instruction for global competence, teachers design learning experiences that invite students to think with and apply concepts, methods, and tools from one or more disciplines to make sense of an issue of global significance. We call such learning experiences *performances of global competence* because they enable students to demonstrate their developing capacity to understand and act on matters of global significance (Boix Mansilla & Gardner, 1998).

Performances of global competence don't need to be staged final exhibitions, as one would see in a theater. Rather, they involve using knowledge and skills to examine or act on a global matter. They can take place at the beginning, middle, or end of a unit. They can range from conducting a thought experiment, to crafting an argument or producing a critique, to comparing data or creating a work of art.

Five capacities are crucial here. Effective performances of global competence do the following.

Use knowledge and skill in and across disciplines in novel situations. Although gaining information about the world is necessary from lectures, books, videos, websites, and other outlets, it's not sufficient for global competence. Performances of global competence give students the opportunity to apply concepts, methods, and ideas from one or more disciplines to novel situations. Such performances may include identifying key qualities of a region's literary styles; creating a graphic of the causes and consequences of outsourcing; writing a reaction to a newspaper article on the role of private business on economic growth; applying biological knowledge about HIV/AIDS to create a survey; or participating in a discussion on the right to shelter, employing data on homeless people from Bangalore, India, and North America. Students cannot accomplish these performances without grounding their responses in one or more disciplines.

Focus on targeted global competences. Because time and resources are so often limited, educators must weigh how various performance options each contribute to advancing students' targeted global competences. Consider the following example: English and Spanish teachers are designing a unit to help students understand the influence that culture and personal experience may have on the work of certain Latin American authors. They brainstorm performances of global competence that can encourage students to recognize global perspectives—a targeted competence for this unit. The teachers must evaluate two possible assignments: either students can write a reflection comparing influences across various Latin American writers on their respective literary styles, or they can organize a class Latin American poetry slam. Teachers opt for the first assignment because it's better aligned with their global competence goal: to help students understand how cultural influences shape literary work among selected poets in Latin America.

Connect students' local experience to the world. Powerful units or projects tend to begin where students are. For example, one high school unit we looked at on outsourcing began by having students look at where the objects they own were produced. Beginning with their personal interests, experiences, and contexts enables students to see the relevance of global issues in their own lives. In so doing, they begin to understand how local experiences can affect and be affected by affairs taking place elsewhere.

Engage students cognitively, socially, and emotionally. Potent performances of global competence engage students in cognitively demanding tasks, such as applying disciplinary constructs to novel situations, conducting inquiries, and explaining perspectives. Likewise, they often demand social interaction, perhaps calling for working in teams to craft a product, finding information through face-to-face interviews, exchanging views with peers living in contexts that differ from their own, engaging in debates, enlisting others' help and support, and participating in community service projects. Social and cognitive engagement produces emotional engagement as well. Students tackle global issues with excitement, joy, compassion, fear, sadness, and anger—emotions that ultimately shape their learning.

It's not uncommon, for instance, for students learning about climate change, extreme poverty, and epidemics to encounter feelings of anguish or despair. The magnitude of these issues can make them feel rather impotent. But such feelings are often followed by the conviction to take action. Experienced global educators must help students work through their feelings of impotence, anger, or fear constructively. For example, they may invite students to articulate their perspectives on an issue, propose solutions to raise awareness among their classmates, or take some concrete action to improve conditions. These activities foster global competence and encourage students to recognize their active membership in a world that extends beyond their immediate environment.

Invite personal synthesis. Performances of global competence may include having students articulate their personal position in an essay or prepare a final research report. Or perhaps teachers will ask students to revisit the journal entries they wrote at the beginning of a unit on a given topic and identify any shifts in thought that have taken place in the interim. Students can synthesize their learning by creating a product; solving a problem; or putting together a campaign, presentation, video, or action project designed to improve conditions.

Performances of Global Competence in Rosa Lin's Earth Science Class

Performances in this unit focus primarily on students' inquiry beyond their local environments. Students begin by examining accounts of the changing climate in multiple world regions. Materials range from scientists' video accounts of changes in the Greenland ice sheet to evidence from ice cores in areas of Africa and South America. Students discuss these events, hypothesizing how the earth system dynamics they have learned about may be involved and brainstorming possible consequences for local populations. Since the beginning of the year, students have been tracking weekly news on a scientific reporting website—a volcanic eruption in Iceland, cyclone alerts in the South Pacific, the rising incidence of skin cancer in New Zealand, and outbreaks of malaria and the West Nile Virus.

Learning to inquire scientifically about planetary changes is a central goal of the course and of this unit in particular. To understand how we know about climatic changes in the past and in the present, students examine the work of paleo-climatologists and engage with current data on sea ice melting. Toward the end of the unit, students in the earth science honors class conduct an independent inquiry project on a local-global planetary change of their choice. They must craft a researchable question, argue for its significance, and identify a database to use in conducting their analysis. Examples of questions include the following: Have precipitation patterns changed around the world (choosing three locations)? Is the spring arriving earlier in the northern United States? Have there been changes in the frequency and intensity of hurricanes? In their papers, students must describe and justify their procedures, present their data and analysis clearly, and include a reflective conclusion and a bibliography with strong, reputable sources.

As the unit unfolds, students often develop a desire to participate in mitigating and adapting to climate change. As the teacher noted,

> It's not enough to teach 9th grade students about earth systems or the causes and consequences of climate change. These kids will want to do something to preserve the earth's balance—they will want to participate.

To meet this urge, the unit concludes with a study of climate solutions. Students learn about energy consumption and production, evaluate the pros and cons of solutions—such as alternative energy sources, nuclear power, green technologies, and environmental architecture—and consider the effect of each on the earth's natural systems.

One year, interested students participated in a video competition. Students produced five- to six-minute videos that captured something important they had learned about climate dynamics, helping viewers understand how to mitigate further change. The videos had to make a strong case for studying climate change around the world through a global earth sciences perspective.

How Will We Know If Students Are Making Progress?

Effective performances of global competence both develop and reveal students' capabilities. But what about assessments? Four qualities are of utmost importance. Such assessments do the following:

- **Focus on global competence**. Assessing student work for global competence involves examining it for what it reveals about how students are able to investigate the world through disciplinary and interdisciplinary study, inquire about topics of global significance, recognize perspectives, communicate ideas, and take action. The matrices included in the Appendix (see p. 142) provide a helpful starting point for teachers in developing criteria to assess global competence in each core competence.

- **Are ongoing.** Because developing global competence is demanding and involves higher-order thinking, teachers need to monitor and support students' learning over time. High-quality assessment therefore begins in the initial days of a unit or course; teachers can invite students to share their thoughts and questions about the global topic under study and gauge their orientations, assumptions, and possible misconceptions.

- **Offer informative feedback**. As experienced teachers know, students need more than a general grade for the quality of their work to excel. They must understand which specific features of their reflection, paper, presentation, or work of art demonstrate their accomplishments and what they need to do for further growth. Having explicit assessment criteria and rubrics is essential here.

- **Can be conducted by multiple stakeholders.** Obviously, teachers hold the primary responsibility for assessing their students' work and offering guidance. However, peers can also do so using established criteria. Likewise, members of the community or experts can offer feedback on student presentations, video productions, or graduation portfolios, thus deepening students' sense of the authenticity of their studies and their engagement in topics that matter well beyond grades, exams, and classrooms.

Assessing Student Progress in Rosa Lin's Earth Science Class

Rosa Lin's assessment criteria align with her goals to help students understand the earth as a dynamic and ever-changing system, appreciate the power of scientific inquiry, participate in caring for our planet, and develop a strong sense of global environmental stewardship. Three excerpts from Lin's unit materials illustrate how she monitors and supports her students' learning. The teacher must do the following:

- **Clarify expectations in assignment descriptions**. Consider Lin's instructions for students' research reports. Figure 7.2 shows how the teacher's expectations and criteria focus on helping students conduct a scientific inquiry of their chosen phenomenon and invite them to monitor their own production against such expectations.

- **Pay attention to learning challenges**. To support students early in their learning process, Lin crafts assignment descriptions that support students' independent work. For example, in Figure 7.3, she goes over how to formulate a good question for study, something students may initially have difficulty with.

- **Target learning goals through ongoing feedback.** Providing specific feedback on early drafts of student work enables Lin to correct misconceptions and support students in producing quality work. Consider her feedback on one student's sea ice melting problem, as shown in Figure 7.4.

Figure 7.2
Criteria for Conducting a Scientific Inquiry

Title: State the specific question. This question is the title of the IRP.
Is this a question? Is it stated clearly? Is it relevant to our efforts to understand local and global changes in the earth? Are there dependent and independent variables?

Background: Review up-to-date literature relevant to the question.
This is a three-page original written paper, one per student, individually graded.
What's the big picture science context that frames the specific question? Is research up-to-date? Is it relevant to the location and focus of your question? Did you find your own sources? Are valid sources cited in the text either using footnotes or numbers referring to the bibliography? *Cite your sources in the text*, using either footnotes or 1, 2, 3, and so on.

Your hypothesis: Write one good paragraph.
What hypothesis will be tested in this experiment? What is the predicted result? Please do not write this *after* you do the experiment. Scientists expect to be wrong along the way; it's how they get closer to getting it right. *What relationship, correlation, and dependence among variables do you expect, based on what you already know?*
Remember, a graph is the story of the relationship among variables, so predict what you expect to find. ("Tiny," "a lot," "a little bit," and "humongous" are not scientific terms.) Quantify based on what you already know. Consider comparisons: Compared with what is something a change?
Consider logic: How does your hypothesis flow from your background paper/research?
Consider clarity: Is your hypothesis simply stated and clear?

This project was designed to answer the question of whether a change in air temperature affects the extent of sea ice. It connects to the bigger question, "How does this affect me?" In fact, this study matters to everyone because if all the ice at the poles disappears, then sea levels will rise and encroach on the land we live on. This is especially of concern in countries that have a border with the sea, given that a large

Figure 7.3

Formulating a Good Question for Study

Independent Inquiry Projects

Inquiry is the intellectual side of science. Inquiry is thinking like a scientist. It's being inquisitive, asking why, and searching for answers. Earth inquiry involves interpreting local problems we choose to study against the background of the earth as a system.

Who asks the question? You do.

Most of the time, focus questions are given to you: Did birds descend from dinosaurs? How have CO_2 levels changed over time? What is the relationship between the amount of water vapor in the atmosphere and rainfall? However, now you can pursue your own focused question.

Asking good questions is one of the hardest challenges in science. You could spend weeks trying to formulate a good question, one that can be answered through experimentation. Scientists often dedicate their lives to searching for the answers to specific questions that pave the way to answering the big burning questions that won't let go.

Your question needs to be specific enough that you can take measurements. What will you measure, in what location, and over what time frame to test your hypothesis? These measurements will be your data. You will need to ensure the accuracy of the data you collect and analyze, interpret, and communicate your results to others. You will need to make sure that your question is manageable. A good researchable question captures the heart of the problem you're choosing to study, as well as key locations and time frames, considering the data available to you.

What will be your question? Consider a few drafts, ask for feedback, and prepare to workshop your questions when we conduct our workshop review.

Figure 7.4

Teacher Feedback on a Student's Question for Study

Your question of study: Has the extent of sea ice changed?

- Your question is too general; give examples of specific countries and regions.
- You say "a large percentage" of people live near the coast. How much, on average, of the world's population lives near the coast? Be precise in your writing about local and global patterns.
- "Sea level rise." Remember that sea ice doesn't add to sea level rise; you should know this from your research. What kind of melting *would* make a difference?

percentage of the population lives on the coast. A decrease in sea ice would also affect other earth spheres; the tree line, for example, would rise, further distorting the delicate balance of the earth systems.

Standards and Accountability

Rosa Lin uses state standards for learning in science to ensure that the scientific concepts, skills, and attitudes her students will encounter in this unit address 9th grade requirements for her state, Massachusetts (see Figure 7.5). She does not teach prescribed concepts and skills in isolation. Rather, she has identified a topic of global significance—climate instability in the earth's system—that naturally lends itself to students' achieving state standards while supporting her global competence learning goals.

Figure 7.5
9th Grade Science Standards, Massachusetts

I. Content Standards

1.8 Read, interpret, and analyze a combination of ground-based observations, satellite data, and computer models to demonstrate earth systems and their interconnections.

Scientific Inquiry Skills Standards

SIS1. Make observations, raise questions, and formulate hypotheses.
SIS2. Design and conduct scientific investigations.
SIS3. Analyze and interpret results of scientific investigations.
SIS4. Communicate and apply the results of scientific investigations.

Mathematical Skills

• Construct and use tables and graphs to interpret data sets.
• Solve simple algebraic expressions.
• Perform basic statistical procedures to analyze the center and spread of data.
• Measure with accuracy and precision.
• Convert within a unit.
• Use common prefixes.
• Use ratio and proportion to solve for problems.

Source: From *Massachusetts Science and Technology/Engineering Curriculum Framework, October 2006.* Copyright 2006 by Massachusetts Department of Education.

Toward the end of the unit, Lin invites students to reflect on their learning, the findings that struck them as significant, and the questions they now have. This process of reflection reveals students' enhanced capacity to inquire about the world beyond their immediate environments. For many, this understanding couples with a desire to make a difference.

In Sum

Not all efforts to teach for global competence need to take the form of an in-depth unit like Rosa Lin's. For example, following a unit on the French Revolution, a teacher in New York decided to run a series of Socratic seminars on the construction of national identity in contemporary France. Using an account of the debate in France banning headscarves in schools, provided by Facing History and Ourselves, the students discuss questions like these: What does it mean to be a French person today? In what ways are the ideals of the French Revolution still alive in today's France, and in what ways are they being challenged? How is being French a matter of law, individual identity, group identity, or birthright? Students deliberate on these issues using primary sources, historical accounts of immigration, policy statements, and public opinion polls. The Socratic seminars last only a few days, but they enable students to revisit the French Revolution with a contemporary global perspective.

Teachers may opt for in-depth units of study or target selected lessons. They may favor introducing a given competence into a course and revisiting it frequently or adding a project on a global issue at the end of a course. Regardless of scope or discipline, instructors benefit from informed and deliberate planning. Designing high-quality instruction is never a linear process. Rather, it's a spiraled process that involves brainstorming, designing, getting feedback, redesigning, testing ideas in practice, reflecting, and redesigning once more. Teachers are well supported in this process by professional learning groups with whom they might share their emerging plans.

Questions to Ponder

- Which of these principles for designing instruction for global competence reflects your typical approach to teaching? Enriches your typical approach to teaching? Puzzles you at this time?

- What qualities of Rosa Lin's unit call your attention and why? What obstacles do educators confront when teaching for global competence? What strategies enable them to overcome such challenges?

- Consider some of the activities your students do. In what ways are they performances of global competence? In what ways could they become performances of global competence?

What Schools Can Do

To become globally competent, students need multiple curricular and extracurricular opportunities to think and act on matters of global significance. What can schools do to create such internationally minded environments?

Clearly, schools begin such efforts at different starting points. Some schools may already be offering international education opportunities. These might include a carefully designed world history course, a successful model United Nations program after school, or a program to mine cultural diversity among immigrant families in the local community.

Fernando Reimers, a Harvard University professor and a leading expert in the field, says that no matter what approach teachers take, they should keep in mind that helping students become globally competent is "serious and rigorous work," not just a nice thing to do. "We're not going to educate global citizens by organizing a food festival in a school once a year in which we celebrate the heritage of all students," Reimers says. "That's nice, but it's not the way we teach physics or trigonometry or literature or history" (Asia Society & OECD, 2018).

This chapter provides a broad framework that can guide educators as they pursue change selectively or transform whole-school structures to promote global competence. Although the framework is drawn largely from schools in the United States, its lessons can be adapted to—and informed by—school change innovations around the world.

Beginning in 2003, the Center for Global Education at Asia Society developed a comprehensive Global School Design (see Figure 8.1). This design, which now belongs to Community Catalyst Partners, serves as a blueprint for the creation of schools that systematically nurture students' inclination to think about and act on issues of global significance.

Figure 8.1
Global School Design Blueprint

Source: Copyright 2021 by Community Catalyst Partners. Reprinted with permission.

The Global School Design serves as a framework to help ensure that all aspects of the school community support a global focus, with the specific intent being to ensure equity in access for all youth.

Six Target Areas That Support Global Learning

Let's briefly review each of the six parts of the framework to see how schools can "globalize" systematically.

Mission, Vision, and Culture

What evidence shows that the school's vision and mission prioritize global competence and equity to support all students' employability and citizenship in a global era? Evidence would include the following:

- The school's mission/vision statements articulate a commitment to the equitable development of global competence for college/career readiness and ethical citizenship.

- All students are engaged in the work of becoming globally competent, and thus they attend school regularly and conduct themselves appropriately.

Student Learning Outcomes

What evidence shows that the school achieves student learning outcomes that prepare students for the global innovation age? Evidence would include the following:

- All students graduate competent in the four domains of global competence: investigating the world, recognizing perspectives, communicating ideas, and taking action.

- Student progress meets or exceeds benchmarks for academic performance.

Curriculum, Instruction, and Assessment

What evidence shows that the school's curriculum, instruction, and assessment align with the four domains of global competence and related performance outcomes? Evidence would include the following:

- The school's curriculum is interconnected across disciplines, aligns with academic benchmarks, and explicitly addresses the development of global competence.

- The school's curriculum references knowledge from and about a broad array of cultures and provides students with multiple opportunities to engage in complex, inquiry-based projects and investigations designed to support mastery of global competence.

School Organization and Governance

What evidence shows that the school actively and equitably engages faculty, staff, students, and parents—both current and prospective—in organizing and governing the school around a global focus? Evidence would include the following:

- The school recruits, hires, and retains a diverse staff whose knowledge or life experiences reflect their interest in global competence.

- Decision-making structures function efficiently and ensure the effective involvement of stakeholders representing the diversity of the school community.

Professional Development

What evidence shows that the school's globally focused professional development programs are available to all faculty and staff and are implemented across the school community? Evidence would include the following:

- School leaders, faculty, and staff continuously focus on understanding and implementing strategies to develop global competence in all students.

- Through the structured sharing of teacher and student work, school leaders, faculty, and staff engage in collaborative analysis and reflection on existing instructional practices to identify potential sources of racial and ethnic bias.

Partnerships

What evidence shows that the school seeks out, cultivates, and nurtures partnerships with students' families and with community individuals and organizations that welcome cultural diversity into the school and enhance a focus on global competence? Evidence would include the following:

- Parents, families, and guardians across the range of racial, ethnic, and religious backgrounds in the school community are actively engaged in the school's work.

- The school develops key partnerships with organizations and institutions that enhance its focus on global competence.

Let's now look at each of these six target areas in more depth.

Mission, Vision, and Culture

A clear signal to students and educators alike that a school prioritizes global competence is a mission statement that says so. For example, the mission statement of the Denver Center for International Studies (n.d.), serving students in grades 6–12, leaves no doubt about its goals for students: "The Denver Center for International Studies prepares students for college by developing multilingual, interculturally competent students who are actively involved in a rapidly changing world."

Similarly, here's how the Mulgrave School (n.d.), an international school in Vancouver, Canada, describes its vision:

> By inspiring excellence—the continuous pursuit of personal best—in education and life, Mulgrave strives to equip lifelong learners to thrive in a culturally diverse and an interdependent world and to embrace, with passion and confidence, their responsibility always to do their best to support others and to make a difference by serving their communities, both locally and in the world at large.

A school's vision and mission can drive the creation of a school culture of global competence, one in which issues of global significance permeate hallway posters, cafeteria discussions, and student work and organizations.

Schools seeking to nurture the core global competences allot them sufficient time. Indeed, establishing a schoolwide culture of global competence involves more than just teaching for global competence; it entails creating an environment where students are acculturated into globally competent ways of thinking and acting, ways that become habits of mind and heart.

Student Learning Outcomes

Developing a graduate profile that describes the specific knowledge, skills, and dispositions that students must acquire by graduation is a powerful way to translate a school's mission into clear expectations. The profile should set out not only how students are expected to perform, but also the kind of people it hopes they will become. For example, a school can indicate clearly how it wants its graduates to value and engage with individuals from different racial, ethnic, and religious backgrounds. Designing a graduate profile is a substantial undertaking, often involving collaboration among educators and the school's broader community. Schools and districts may find it useful to take an existing graduate profile and customize it.

The International Studies Schools Network (ISSN), initially developed by Asia Society and now run by Community Catalyst Partners, is a group of more than 70 schools that, since 2004, has worked to implement the Global School Design. Schools might wish to adapt its Graduate Profile (Asia Society, n.d.), which specifies the following:

- **Our graduates are ready for college:**
  - They earn a high school diploma by completing a college-preparatory, globally focused course of study requiring the demonstration of college-level work across the curriculum.
  - They have the experience of achieving expertise by researching, understanding, and developing new knowledge about a world culture or an internationally relevant issue.
  - They learn how to manage their own learning by identifying options, evaluating opportunities, and organizing educational experiences that will enable them to work and live in a global society.
  - They graduate with all options open for postsecondary education, work, and service.

- **Our graduates have the knowledge required in the global era:**
  - They understand mathematics as a universal way to make sense of the world and solve complex, authentic problems, communicating their understandings using the symbols, language, and conventions of the subject.
  - They understand crucial scientific concepts, engage in scientific reasoning, and apply the processes of scientific inquiry to understand the world and explore possible solutions to global problems.
  - They understand how the geography of natural and manmade phenomena influences both cultural development and historical and contemporary world events.
  - They understand the history of major world events and cultures and use this understanding to analyze and interpret contemporary world issues.
  - They understand arts and literature and how to use them as lenses through which to view nature, society, and culture, as well as to express ideas and emotions.

- **Our graduates are skilled for success in a global environment:**
  - They are "literate for the 21st century"; they are proficient in reading, writing, viewing, listening, and speaking in English and in one or more other world languages.
  - They demonstrate creative and complex thinking and problem-solving skills by analyzing and producing viable solutions to problems with no known or single right answer.
  - They use digital media and technology to access and evaluate information from around the world and effectively communicate, synthesize, and create new knowledge.
  - They make healthy decisions that enhance their physical, mental, and emotional well-being.

- **Our graduates are connected to the world:**
  - They effectively collaborate with individuals from different cultural backgrounds and respect people from other racial, cultural, and religious groups as they would have others respect their own.
  - They analyze and evaluate global issues from multiple perspectives.

- They understand how the world's people and institutions are interconnected and how crucial international economic, political, technological, environmental, and social systems operate interdependently across nations and regions.
- They accept the responsibilities of global citizenship and make ethical decisions and responsible choices that contribute to the development of a more just, peaceful, and sustainable world.

In best-case scenarios, faculty members and the school community use the vision and mission of a school along with the graduate profile as ongoing tools to evaluate the school's intellectual and social climate and monitor student progress. They are included in the school handbook; referred to in discussions among school faculty, students, parents, and partners; and appear in communications coming from the school and posted on its website. Moreover, a system is in place to ensure that the school periodically reevaluates these guides to ensure their relevance within an ever-changing global environment.

Curriculum, Instruction, and Assessment

A school's approach to articulating the curriculum and engaging students in instruction and assessment are the primary ways through which global competence becomes a reality for students. Let's look at how each of these elements of a school's core work can promote global competence.

Curriculum

A variety of approaches, such as those that follow, put teaching and learning for global competence within the reach of every school.

Engaging students by addressing global challenges. Across disciplines, students become deeply engaged in subject matter when they see its relevance to solving major problems in the world or creating new opportunities for improving conditions. For example, in a high school biochemistry course, students might explore the energy value of foods through the lens of hunger and food scarcity in the world. In mathematics, even young children can begin to learn how numbers and mathematical expressions help people understand the world, from the size of populations to the sequencing of events that helps illuminate the path of history. Students can study key concepts in social studies, such as migration and urbanization, on the global scale, and the arts provide unlimited opportunities for examining global issues and producing creative responses. Teaching for global competence involves finding meaningful new ways to reframe the content teachers already cover, avoiding contrived or superficial connections.

A number of organizations provide resources for teachers to support student inquiry into issues of global importance. For example, the GeoChallenge is an annual themed and standards-based competition from the National Geographic Society (2020) that challenges student groups in grades 5 through 8 across the United States to develop a creative solution to a real-world problem. A recent challenge—Tackling Plastic!—invited students to investigate the urgent issue of plastic pollution in our waterways.

Globalizing the context for learning. Viewing course content from a global perspective provides important opportunities to deepen understanding and hone critical reasoning skills. A question such as this—How have individuals or governments abroad influenced or been influenced by developments in U.S. history?—invites students to take a global perspective in a U.S. history course. Likewise, English language arts courses might include works from around the world that expose students to the perspectives and experiences of people from myriad cultural backgrounds. Especially for children of color, finding people who "look like me" across the curriculum can help develop a positive sense of racial and cultural identity while enhancing interest and engagement in their studies.

Comparative analysis provides especially fertile ground for recognizing and weighing perspectives. For instance, students learning about revolutions could compare the Russian Revolution of 1917 with the French Revolution of 1789 and the Arab Spring of 2011. Similarly, students might examine international efforts to mitigate climate change by conducting an analysis of three different countries' policies, examining original documents from those countries. They could enrich their analysis by considering public opinion garnered from the newspapers of the countries in question on those climate change policies. Students could also examine important questions deeply relevant to their lives, such as, What are the causes and consequences of systemic racialized oppression from historical and contemporary perspectives in the United States, Europe, Asia, and elsewhere?

Connecting to universal themes. Broadening the base of literature that students are exposed to helps them discover universal themes, such as the search for identity, the effect of oppression, or the power of the individual to change the course of history. This is clearly evident in the work of Lezama Lima, a poet we looked at earlier, who wrote about disappointment, religion, sacrifice, and femininity, among other topics. In social studies, powerful questions—such as, Why is religion a universal phenomenon?—can lead students to a fascinating analysis of beliefs, rituals, and traditions of the world's religions.

Michael Jones, a high school social studies teacher in Naperville, Illinois, had his students research a religious issue in a global context as a final assignment one year. Students had to connect with someone who had direct experience with the issue they were investigating. Then each student had to show what he or she learned by creating a piece of art, a movie, a written paper, an awareness campaign, a children's book, or some other artifact. Whatever they produced had to be critiqued by the person they had spoken with.

"It's a different thing to write a paper on religious intolerance and then have it critiqued by a Pakistani imam who has been a victim of that intolerance," Jones says. After completing the project, the students had to use what they produced with a real-world audience. One group, for example, wrote a children's book on anti-Semitism, had it reviewed by two experts, and then read it to younger children (Asia Society & OECD, 2018).

Illuminating the global history of knowledge. Mathematics and science are particularly amenable to demonstrating the global historical roots of knowledge and its progression over time through global interactions. Young children can explore the origins of counting across ancient civilizations in Mesopotamia, Africa, and the Americas to connect the history of mathematics to what is taught today. For example, Hindu and Chinese mathematicians discovered Pascal's triangle long before Pascal was born. Scientific knowledge and modes of inquiry that traveled along trade routes in the Islamic world 1,000 years ago are part of the heritage of ideas and discoveries leading to today's universal methods of scientific inquiry and standards of evidence.

Learning through international collaboration. Videoconferencing, social networking, and other communication technologies now give students unprecedented opportunities to investigate issues of global significance with students around the world, much the way working professionals now operate in global teams. There are a great many ways to structure such interactions among students, from scientific collaborations on shared databases to collaborative artistic endeavors. As just one example practicable almost anywhere, inviting community members into a school to share the multinational origins of everyday retail products can be an eye-opening experience for students.

Opportunities for students to learn from adults worldwide through virtual connections are also widely accessible through universities, learned organizations, nonprofits, and businesses. iEARN (www.iearn .org), a nonprofit organization made up of more than 30,000 schools and youth organizations in more than 140 countries, empowers teachers and young people to work together online using the internet and other new communications technologies. More than 2 million students each day are engaged in collaborative project work worldwide.

Instruction

In terms of instruction, Rosa Lin's unit on global climate change illustrates how teachers can use core knowledge, skills, and competences to address a problem that students, teachers, and society deem of global import. Lin's approach represents one form of project-based instruction. Properly structured, project-based instruction is a valuable tool for engaging students across racial and cultural lines, a proven approach to undermine prejudice, and a promoter of prosocial attitudes.

The Center for Global Education at Asia Society (n.d.) has created a framework to facilitate project-based learning using the acronym SAGE (**S**tudent choice, **A**uthentic work, **G**lobal significance, **E**xhibition to a real audience):

- **Student choice.** Students should be able to make choices about how to carry out their projects, which requires teachers to be clear about their expectations and students to take responsibility for their learning. Giving students choices enables them to take ownership of the project and deepens their engagement.

- **Authentic work.** The projects should provide a range of authentic experiences that are modeled after how globally competent professionals would carry out such a project in the real world outside the classroom.

- **Global significance.** Students should apply what they have learned through disciplinary studies to relevant, real-life issues. This will help them develop the habits as well as the motivation to act in productive ways to address world problems.

- **Exhibition to a real audience.** Students should then have the opportunity to exhibit their work and demonstrate what they have learned to a real audience that will give them meaningful feedback they can use to improve.

An area of instruction proving to be fertile ground for promoting global competence is career and technical education (CTE). Anchored in preparing students for the careers of their choice and focused on the crucial academic, technical, and employability skills needed for success, CTE offers a natural platform on which to build global competencies. Globally minded CTE programs can provide the rigorous and authentic setting necessary to prepare students for the competitive world economy, while offering a more engaging, motivating, and relevant education experience.

For example, a high school in Seattle, Washington, requires freshmen to take a semester of global health. The teacher, Donavyn Thomas, uses a project-based learning approach to cover such topics as communicable and noncommunicable disease, policies of the World Health Organization, major global health problems, and issue awareness and advocacy. Students work on case studies and real-world problems and present to classmates in order to hone their work before presenting it to other audiences. According to Thomas, "Global Health really opens up the students' minds to what's going on in health, not only in our community, but around the world. It's difficult for them to shift their thinking away from themselves and toward others, but they now think of health in a new way" (Asia Society & Longview Foundation, 2016).

Assessment

Over the past decade, states have collaborated to develop new forms of assessments that are linked closely to the Common Core State Standards. Just as schools need standards-based summative assessments to measure aspects of learning crucial to global competency, they also need to use various formative and summative assessments to enable students to demonstrate their global competence.

Schools in the International Studies Schools Network incorporate performance-based assessment across all grade levels and subject areas. A set of performance outcomes and related rubrics have been designed for each academic content area, as well as for a set of cross-cutting *global leadership skills*, which describe characteristics of student work that demonstrate both college readiness and global competence. Teachers may use these performance outcomes and rubrics as starting points for designing performance assessment tasks.

Lasting from a few days to several weeks, a performance task requires students to investigate a global problem and construct a solution reflecting diverse perspectives through the application of knowledge and skills derived from rigorous disciplinary or interdisciplinary study. The work is then scored against the rubrics and feedback is provided so that students see clearly where they need to improve to meet the criteria for global competence and college readiness in each subject area and on the global leadership competences.

In addition, the process of assessing the work can be powerful in helping teachers improve their instructional practice. How does the work that students produced differ from what the teacher expected while crafting the task? What does the work say about possible gaps in students' knowledge and skills? These are the kinds of useful questions resulting from careful examination of student work. As such, performance-based assessment is a key *instructional* strategy. It supports teachers in designing and refining instructional units and related assessments that enable students to demonstrate the complex skills of global competence, while also facilitating the continuous process of pedagogical improvement for teachers.

World Languages

The study of world languages is a core component of global competence and is therefore an especially important aspect of curriculum, instruction, and assessment within the overall school design. Virtually all of the highest-performing nations in the world require their students to begin sustained second language instruction from an early age. Yet according to the American Councils for International Education (2017), only 20 percent of K–12 students in the United States are enrolled in a foreign language course.

The failure to embrace the benefits of world language programs in the United States stems, in part, from a failure to recognize the ways that learning another language contributes to a student's broader academic and professional skill set. Learning a second language is one of the most effective ways for students to see things from multiple perspectives and consider worldviews that might differ from their own. And although there is much debate over which languages are the most crucial to learn, research shows that the skills students develop learning one language can be applied to learning others. The goal, therefore, should be to make students effective learners of *language in general*, rather than just successful learners of one language in particular.

Although the mastery of grammar and vocabulary have formed the core of most world language instruction in the United States, the best programs go beyond language proficiency to develop students' global competence. Sustainable programs connect with other academic disciplines, engage the larger school community, and offer opportunities to interact with students in other countries through electronic exchanges, travel, or studying abroad.

For example, world language students can compare the target language and culture with their own language and culture, developing a stronger understanding of differing perspectives, as well as of the general principles of language patterns and structure. Students can communicate with diverse audiences that include native speakers of the language and use their developing skills in authentic contexts. Indeed, building connections with native speakers makes the learning experience more authentic—and these personal relationships can motivate students to continue their language study over the long term.

Starting at an early age is the best way to ensure that students will develop significant levels of proficiency in a language and speak it without a heavy accent and interference from their first language. But starting early is not enough. Many elementary language immersion programs currently feed into middle and high schools that don't offer a robust slate of world languages, forcing students to stop developing their proficiency. Similarly, many programs start early but only offer students a relatively small number of contact hours each week. Although this exposure is certainly better than nothing, it's unlikely to significantly improve student proficiency. Students need substantial, continuous instruction from the early grades on to reach their full potential as world language learners.

A key consideration in making a language program compelling is incorporating tasks that involve higher-order cognitive skills even at the beginning levels. For example, rather than just having students memorize grammar patterns or vocabulary, teachers can ask them to analyze and extract those patterns from authentic materials, such as newspapers and magazines. Similarly, teachers can incorporate interactive games and role-playing scenarios that simulate real-world situations, asking students to compare the target language and culture with their own.

Another mechanism for building student engagement is to incorporate content from other areas of instruction into the language classroom. Teaching lessons in the target language that connect to students' science or history courses, for example, is a great way to make the language more relevant and interesting. The ultimate goal is for students to develop their communication skills in the language, learn and think about languages and cultures more broadly, and apply their newfound skills in the real world.

School Organization and Governance

When students are genuinely engaged in investigating the world, they often encounter challenging ideas, unsettling facts, intriguing opinions, and divergent values. Protests against racially targeted police brutality, for example, raise strong feelings among both children of color and white students. It's therefore imperative for school cultures to foster trusting relationships among students and faculty members. Creating cultures of trust doesn't just happen. They are the product of organizational structures that maximize opportunities for teachers and students to communicate honestly and develop authentic and appropriate personal relationships. Such cultures also flourish when students have a voice in how they learn and other aspects of how the school functions.

To build relationships that nurture global competence, teachers and administrators may ask the following questions:

- How comfortable are students initiating meaningful conversations with their advisors, faculty members, or other students about issues of global significance, especially those that touch close to home in students' lives?

- Are mechanisms in place, such as an advisory program, that provide safe spaces for students to develop both their academic and personal voices on global concerns?

- Do students have frequent opportunities to encounter individuals from backgrounds different from their own in ways that promote tolerance and understanding?

Developing global competence is not solely an academic enterprise; it's a way of acting and being in the world with others that values collaboration and inclusion. In an informal focus group discussion at the Academy for International Studies (AIS) in Charlotte, North Carolina, a student expressed the connection between the global and the personal in these words:

> Most people at AIS are really friendly and open. They're eager to learn about different [cultures], and they're very accepting of people, regardless of whatever background [they're from]. I'm sure there are little groups within AIS but…if anybody were to talk bad about someone, we would all come together and be like, "No. This is AIS, we're more than that." So…in the end, we're like a big family. Families have their problems, and they may not agree on some things or clash, but in the end, we're all going to have each other's back.

Relationships within the classroom should reflect the values of global competence. Teachers should help students establish norms and routines that stress the importance of respect for one another based on the capacity to understand and appreciate different perspectives and life experiences. Teachers can influence students' perceptions of one another by whom they call on, whom they select for classroom duties, how they create teams for projects, and how they design a seating plan.

They can search out multiethnic and multicultural examples to illustrate concepts and principles in the curriculum, emphasizing the contributions of people from different countries and different heritages. Doing this requires a capacity to reflect on one's own perspectives on race, ethnicity, social class, gender identification, and other student characteristics that bring a rich diversity to classrooms; however, this may also trigger implicit biases antithetical to the core value of equity inherent in global competence. Fostering global competence in youth requires developing global competence in their teachers.

Professional Development

No matter how deep their passion for developing globally competent students, teachers cannot teach what they do not know. Teachers need ongoing opportunities to develop their own global competence, as well as the pedagogical capacities to foster global competence in their students. Asia Society's *Going Global: Preparing Our Students for an Interconnected World* (2008) presents a useful framework. Globally focused professional development should do the following:

- Show teachers how to integrate global content and foster global competence.

- Bring other cultures into the school in ways that are meaningful for students and faculty and that align with the goals of the program. Resources include university-based Title VI centers, which receive federal funds to promote the study of Asia, Africa, Canada, Eastern Europe, Inner Asia, Latin America, the Middle East, Pacific Islands, Russia, and Western Europe and offer conference and workshop opportunities, as well as online cultural resources.

- Offer engaging activities, such as international book clubs, collaborative curriculum development, simulation experiences, and experiential learning opportunities.

- Help teachers develop a rich body of resources for their classrooms, from compiling foreign books, films, and magazines; to selecting informative websites; to engaging a cadre of individuals to serve as advisors.

- Offer frequent opportunities for teacher reflection, such as collaboratively looking at student work using established protocols.

- Support teachers' international travel. There's no substitute for actual international experience to develop globally minded teachers. Many funding opportunities are available through Fulbright scholarships and a range of other programs. To make the most out of teacher travel, schools should offer strong preparation for the travel and have teachers engage in a debriefing process afterward that enables them to make meaning of the experience and consider how to effectively translate it into learning activities for students.

Partnerships

Parents' diverse cultural and linguistic backgrounds are valuable assets waiting to be mined for the benefit of the school community. A simple way to gather relevant information—and signal the value of such information—is to send home a parent inventory form in which parents note their cultural background, languages, interests, and expertise. Teachers can draw on this database to broaden the curriculum with parents' lived experience.

Businesses, universities, museums, cultural organizations, and even retail stores are all important resources in supporting a school's global mission. Businesses may financially support various programs and offer globally focused student internship opportunities. Among myriad potential partner organizations in a community, World Affairs Councils of America (www.worldaffairscouncils.org) can be a particularly important resource for guest speakers and international connections. In addition, students can play a role in identifying the community's key cultural and international resources, mapping them geographically, and organizing them as a searchable database that parallels the asset map of parents' global knowledge and skills.

In Sum

At its core, educating for global competence means creating a school culture where investigating the world is common practice. Such environments recognize racial, cultural, religious, class, and regional perspectives, not only when students address a historical event or a work of literature, but also when they interact informally with teachers and peers. In turn, communicating ideas across diversity occurs not only in Spanish or French class presentations, but also as students resolve a misunderstanding in the hallway. Taking action happens not only in geography class, where students consider options to respond to a distant natural disaster, but also as they self-organize to support a chosen cause. Creating a genuine, equitable culture of global competence involves considering carefully at every turn how to connect the school to its global mission.

Questions to Ponder

- In what ways is your school already developing an equitable culture of global competence? How can you build on these beginnings?

- How can your school creatively use the state standards to promote global competence across the curriculum? Where are the key leverage points?

- How can your school create professional development opportunities to support teaching for global competence and foster teachers' development of cultural competence and humility?

Advocating Through Public Policy

There's a growing movement to ensure that today's students are successful in the global economic and civic environments of the 21st century. Teachers and schools are creatively introducing ways for students to analyze globally significant issues from a variety of perspectives, use international sources, and collaborate across cultures to produce evidence-based arguments and solutions. National and regional government authorities have also initiated programs to promote international education, often focused on the Sustainable Development Goals, that develop cross-cultural knowledge and perspectives. The task ahead is to take these nascent efforts to scale by making global competence a significant component of education and workforce development policy. Developing global competence in *all* students, not just a select few, will require initiating systematic and aligned action at the local, regional, and national levels.

Just as successful businesses benchmark themselves against the best in the world, successful schools look to the best *international* benchmarks for global competence from the highest-performing countries. The Programme for International Student Assessment (PISA) and other international assessments provide important mechanisms for identifying high-performing countries and the policies that support their students' achievement. Benchmarking education policies and approaches to reform provides valuable lessons on what other countries are doing to ensure student achievement and to help them learn about the world and how it works.

This chapter draws on lessons learned from policy reforms implemented by high-performing nations. It proposes promoting global competence as a policy priority through three key strategies: redefining standards and high school graduation requirements, increasing educators' capacity to teach about the world, and providing greater opportunities for students to connect worldwide.

Redefining Standards and High School Graduation Requirements to Include Global Competence

Education systems worldwide face two intertwined challenges. The first is overcoming the chronic failure of school systems to educate all students to high levels, especially students from low-income and ethnic minority backgrounds. The second is preparing students for work and civic roles in a globalized environment, where success increasingly requires the ability to compete, connect, and cooperate on an international scale.

The experience of high-performing regions provides important insights into how U.S. and other education systems can address these two problems. For one thing, high-performing education systems are premised on the belief that all students are capable of achieving at a high level—and that it's necessary that they do so. They understand that education is the way to advancement for students of all ethnic backgrounds and ranges of ability and that hard work and effort, not inherited intelligence, are the keys to success in school.

PISA consistently shows that poverty is not destiny. In PISA 2018, on average across OECD countries, 1 in 10 socioeconomically disadvantaged students performed in the top quarter of reading performance in their country (OECD, 2019). In Australia, Canada, Estonia, Hong Kong (China), Ireland, Macao (China), and the United Kingdom—all of which scored above the OECD average—more than 13 percent of disadvantaged students were academically resilient, meaning that they scored among the top quarter of students in all participating countries/economies, despite the odds against them.

High-performing education systems ensure excellence and equity by setting high, universal standards and driving teaching and learning toward developing the kind of complex thinking skills and engagement with disciplinary content that serve as foundations for global competence. They consistently challenge their students to develop the inductive and deductive reasoning skills they need to investigate the world, to develop the ability to compare viewpoints and recognize multiple perspectives, and to develop world language skills to communicate ideas across diverse audiences, beginning at an early age.

In Singapore, for example, the Framework for 21st Century Competencies formalized by the Ministry of Education in 2010 "underpin[s] the holistic education that our schools provide to better prepare our students for the future" (Singapore Ministry of Education, 2021). Affectionately called the "Swiss roll," the framework has three concentric layers (see www.moe.gov.sg/education-in-sg/21st-century-competencies). At the core are values that define character and shape the beliefs, attitudes, and actions of a person. These values include respect, responsibility, resilience, integrity, care, and harmony. The middle ring signifies social and emotional competencies—the skills children need to manage their emotions, care for others, make responsible decisions, establish positive relationships, and handle challenging situations effectively. The outer ring represents emerging 21st century competencies: civic literacy; global awareness and cross-cultural skills; critical and inventive thinking; and communication, collaboration, and information skills. Since its inception, the 21st century competencies framework is reflected in Singapore's academic curriculum, co-curricular activities, character and citizenship education, and applied learning programs.

The U.S. Department of Education (USDOE; 2018) has also recognized the value of global competence, noting that

> Today more than ever, an effective domestic education agenda must aim to develop a globally and culturally competent citizenry. It is not enough to focus solely on reading, writing, mathematics, and science skills. Today's world also requires critical thinking and creativity to solve complex problems; well-honed communication skills; the ability to speak world languages; and advanced mathematics, science, and technical skills.

To guide educators in advancing global education, the U.S. Department of Education produced a useful framework that emphasizes the development of empathy, collaboration, and other socioemotional skills (see Figure 9.1).

Expectations for what students will learn and be able to do are codified within curriculum guidelines, as well as in disciplinary and cross-cutting standards. At their best, such standards define rigorous and engaging course content, establish coherence, reduce curricular overlap across grade levels, and reduce inequities in curricula across socioeconomic and ethnic groups. The Common Core State Standards reflect the logic of high, systemwide standards, and many U.S. states have adopted them. States opting to update their own standards should seize the opportunity to set standards that promote global competence.

Equally important to establishing high systemwide standards and related assessment systems are efforts to recast and modernize secondary school graduation requirements to include global competence. In the United States, at least 11 states have included global knowledge and skills in their state standards or graduation requirements (Longview Foundation, n.d.-c). Such requirements can include expectations for proficiency in world languages and the capacity to demonstrate global competence across the curriculum.

A related strategy gaining momentum is enabling students to earn certification in global competence through specific course work and experiential learning activities. The Illinois Global Scholar Initiative (https://global-illinois.org), which has been codified into state law, is one of the more long-standing state certificate programs. It has four key requirements:

- **Global coursework.** Students complete a minimum of eight courses with strong global content selected by individual school districts from a broad range of disciplines.

- **Global service learning.** Students engage in at least one sustained, globally focused service learning activity, program, or project approved by the school district.

- **Global collaboration or dialogue.** Students collaborate with global experts or peers through virtual or in-person dialogue or on collaborative projects.

Figure 9.1

U.S. Department of Education Framework for Global Competence

Framework for Developing Global and Cultural Competencies to Advance Equity, Excellence and Economic Competitiveness					
From Early Learning to Careers					
	Early Learning	Elementary	Secondary	Postsecondary	Globally and Culturally Competent Individuals
Collaboration and Communication	Emerging socio-emotional skill building—focus on empathy, cooperation, and problem solving	Progressive socio-emotional skill building—focus on empathy, perspective taking, and conflict management	Strong socio-emotional and leadership skills—emphasis on multicultural understanding and working with diverse groups	Advanced socio-emotional and leadership skills, ability to effectively collaborate and communicate with people in cross-cultural settings	Proficient in at least two languages; Aware of differences that exist between cultures, open to diverse perspectives, and appreciative of insight gained through open cultural exchange; Critical and creative thinkers, who can apply understanding of diverse cultures, beliefs, economies, technology and forms of government in order to work effectively in cross-cultural settings to address societal, environmental or entrepreneurial challenges; Able to operate at a professional level in intercultural and international contexts and to continue to develop new skills and harness technology to support continued growth.
World and Heritage Languages	Developing language skills in English and other languages	Basic proficiency in at least one other language	Proficiency in at least one other language	Advanced proficiency—ability to work or study in at least one other language	
Diverse Perspectives	Emerging global awareness through exposure to diverse cultures, histories, languages, and perspectives	Deepening global awareness through continued exposure to diverse cultures, histories, languages, and perspectives	Deepening local and global knowledge and understanding, including through classes, projects, study abroad, and virtual exchange	Highly developed ability to analyze and reflect on issues from diverse perspectives	
Civic and Global Engagement	Growing awareness of community and institutions	Age-appropriate civic engagement and learning	Demonstrated ability to engage in key civic and global issues	Demonstrated ability for meaningful engagement in a wide range of civic and global issues and to be successful in one's own discipline/specialty in a global context	
Foundation of Discipline-Specific Knowledge and Understanding					

Source: From *Succeeding Globally Through International Education and Engagement* (p. 4), 2018, U.S. Department of Education.

- **Performance-based capstone assessment task.** Students complete the Illinois Global Scholar Performance-Based Assessment, which asks them to investigate and take action to improve a global concern. (Global Education Certificate, 2021)

To support states in developing a comprehensive global education plan, the Center for Global Education at Asia Society and the Longview Foundation developed the International Education Planning Rubric: State Strategies to Prepare Globally Competent Students (Longview Foundation, n.d.-a). The rubric enables states to assess and improve current practice in curriculum, instruction, and assessment; in graduation requirements; in staffing and teacher preparation; and more. Schools and districts could readily adapt the seminal practices framed in the rubric to improve teacher development programs worldwide.

School systems could also conduct an academic and a program audit of current efforts to teach about the world and consider how to infuse international content into existing courses. Such efforts should ensure that the curriculum represents the perspectives and experiences of broadly diverse societies, including those often marginalized in narratives advanced by dominant cultures. Promoting excellence and equity also means increasing the number of students from all backgrounds taking internationally oriented courses, as well as relevant advanced placement courses.

School systems can use global competence as a focused approach to transforming poor-performing schools or creating new schools that promote improved student achievement. For example, schools in Asia Society's International Studies Schools Network have demonstrated marked success in preparing low-income minority students to be both college ready and globally competent by integrating global content across the curriculum and in approaches to instruction and assessment.

Increasing Educators' Capacity to Teach About the World and to Diverse Student Groups

High-performing nations build their human resource systems by focusing energy upfront—in recruiting, preparing, and supporting good teachers—rather than on the back end through reducing teacher attrition and firing weak teachers. Teachers receive good compensation, and their initial preparation includes ample experience in clinical settings. As far as work conditions are concerned, teachers are treated like professionals, they have multiple opportunities to work with colleagues, and they can move up a designated career ladder. Regular, effective professional development focuses on the challenges teachers face, such as developing students' capacity for success in an interdependent world, and teacher evaluation provides useful feedback to improve the quality of instruction.

In the United States, to drive change in teacher preparation programs, states can use their teacher certification mechanisms to outline goals for developing teachers' global competence. Preparation programs should provide better linkages between arts and sciences departments and colleges of education, expanded opportunities for study and teaching abroad for prospective teachers, and systematic training in how to integrate international content and perspectives into required education courses.

The Longview Foundation (n.d.-b) finds that U.S. teacher preparation programs that have been internationalized share the following characteristics:

- General education coursework helps each prospective teacher develop deep knowledge of at least one world region, culture, or global issue and facility in one language in addition to English.

- Professional education courses teach the pedagogical skills to enable future teachers to teach the global dimensions of their subject matter.

- Field experiences for faculty and students support the development of preservice teachers' global perspectives.

- Teachers are well prepared to teach less commonly taught languages, and they update language education pedagogy on the basis of current research and best practice.

- Incentives encourage faculty to engage in this work.

- Teacher preparation courses use formative and summative assessments to evaluate the effectiveness of new strategies in developing the global competence of prospective teachers.

- Training integrates technology into the student experience to enhance instructional practice and facilitate connections to the world.

- Prerequisites for language study are in place, as well as opportunities to build further proficiency during student teachers' course of study.

- Key partnerships are in place, and larger reform initiatives reflect campus and college strategic plans.

- All work aligns to the global aspects of the college and campus strategic vision.

High-performing nations are increasingly devolving authority to meet their national standards to the school level. Thus, the capacity of school principals and lead teachers is ever more crucial. School leaders are fundamental to promoting global competence. They are responsible for establishing the knowledge, skills, and values foundational to global competence as key learning objectives and supporting teachers in their efforts to integrate these objectives as they work to ensure that all students meet local and national learning standards.

Improving the quality of teaching and school leadership may at times require specific, targeted interventions. In his examination of PISA 2018 results, Andreas Schleicher (2019), director for the Directorate of Education and Skills at OECD, noted the following:

> Singapore sends its best teachers to work with the students who are having the greatest difficulty meeting Singapore's high standards. In Japan, officials in prefectural offices will transfer effective teachers to schools with weak faculties to make sure that all students have equally capable instructors. Shanghai has established a system of financial transfer payments to schools serving disadvantaged students and career structures that incentivize high-performing teachers to teach in disadvantaged schools. Shanghai also pairs high-performing districts and schools with low-performing districts and schools, so that the authorities in each can exchange and discuss their development plans with each other and institutes for teachers' professional development can share their

curricula, teaching materials, and good practices. The government commissions "strong" public schools to take over the administration of "weak" ones by having the "strong" school appoint one of its experienced leaders, such as the deputy principal, to be the principal of the "weak" school and sending a team of experienced teachers to lead in teaching. The underlying expectation is that the ethos, management style, and teaching methods of the high-performing school can be transferred to the poorer-performing school. (p. 23)

The Toronto District School Board: A Case Study

Achieving equitable outcomes for students across ethnic, religious, and socioeconomic lines, including in the development of global knowledge and skills, is a stated goal for nearly every school system. Achieving this goal may require extraordinary efforts, especially when the system has had a history of inequitable results. The Toronto District School Board (TDSB) in Ontario, Canada, addresses systemic inequalities by challenging head-on the discriminatory attitudes, practices, and policies causing the problem.

TDSB is the most diverse school system in Canada. It prides itself on being part of Ontario, one of the highest-performing provinces in Canada, contributing substantially to the nation's top-10 ranking in the world for average math, reading, and science scores on the 2018 PISA. Yet the system has not been successful for all its students, especially those of color.

TDSB's overall high performance was driven by a sustained effort started nearly 20 years ago by the Ontario Ministry of Education to improve results throughout the province, with particular focus on improving the quality of teaching. Although equity was a goal from the start, it took on greater urgency with the release of a 2017 report from the Enhancing Equity Task Force (Toronto District School Board, 2017), a group independent of TDSB that reviewed the district's progress. The report showed that troubling gaps existed in performance by race and ethnicity and that barriers to access to high-quality learning were endemic throughout the system.

In response, the leadership of TDSB redesigned school improvement processes. According to Director of Education John Malloy, "We put our truths on the table" by acknowledging that the rhetoric of equity masked the reality of practice. "As leaders, are we uncomfortable enough to do something different?" he asked. "Our equity work can become complacent, we need the language of anti-oppression to motivate action…. Our learning culture hasn't changed centuries of oppression" (Jackson, 2020).

Willing to name the problem as sustained systemic oppression, the TDSB leadership relied heavily on the extensive data collected on students to uncover how that oppression occurs. For example, while celebrating its 86 percent on-time graduation rate, the focus shifted to the 14 percent of students who were underperforming. Who were they in kindergarten? Who wasn't reading by grade 1? Who was placed in special education by grade 3? Who was being suspended by grade 6? Who was not invited to the academic, college-bound track by grade 9? The data showed clearly that children of color, especially Black students, were overrepresented among those not achieving key milestones in their learning journey.

Using data to illuminate systemic inequities and summoning the courage to confront the roots of the problems have led to important "interruptions" in practices within TDSB. For example, school leaders questioned the validity of the special education system by asking whether there was a racialized component: are only some students, especially racialized students, being identified with special needs? As a result, they are eliminating many special education classes, ending a practice that had effectively shut out disproportionately high numbers of Black students from engaging in the mainstream curriculum.

TDSB's policies ultimately find expression at the school level. Mirroring the systemwide use of data to illuminate inequities, school principals are guided in using their own school's data to ask tough questions about differences in performance by race and ethnicity and to plan sustainable changes to achieve more equitable results.

The system's efforts to dismantle racism and oppression and promote high-achieving, globally competent youth regardless of background are still a work in progress. It is nevertheless a unique approach to addressing attitudinal and structural barriers and developing culturally responsive practice.

Providing Opportunities for Students to Connect Worldwide

Imagine if every school had an ongoing partnership with a school in another part of the world so students could learn with and about one another. Although that may be some years away, organizations such as iEARN, Global Kids (https://globalkids.org), Taking IT Global (www.tigweb.org), and World Savvy (www.worldsavvy.org) are already seizing the opportunity to link young minds. These organizations are eager to partner with schools and school systems in the United States and globally, and their rapid growth speaks to the timeliness of their vision.

Local business, cultural, and nonprofit organizations can support a school system's international work, and international partnerships can directly support efforts to develop global competence. For instance, the Stevens Initiative (www.stevensinitiative.org) is an international effort to build career and global competence skills in young people in the United States, the Middle East, and North Africa by growing and enhancing the field of virtual exchange. The initiative supports educators in developing collaborative learning programs and students' use of a variety of technology tools to connect with one another in real time and asynchronously.

In Sum

High-performing nations are systematically implementing policies and practices that advance the ability of *all* their students to perform in the global economy, evincing a relentless pursuit of excellence and equity in a global era. Giving students the knowledge, skills, values, and perspectives they will need to function successfully in the global age is a task requiring leadership at every level. From national to regional to local school systems, the cost of "putting the *world* into *world-class education*" will be considerable in terms of the time and talent required to integrate a global focus across the curriculum. However, the cost of not doing so will be infinitely greater.

Questions to Ponder

- Do policymakers in your district or state regard global competence as a key priority in education? What's needed to make the case that it should be?

- How do practices and policies in your district or state compare with those of high-performing school systems worldwide?

- What changes in district or state education policy now under consideration could provide a platform for advancing global competence for all students?

What You Can Do

Two decades into the 21st century, a virus first identified in Asia spreads to every corner of the globe, infecting more than 70 million people and disrupting economies, education, and virtually every aspect of everyday life, and requires the most extensive global vaccination effort the world has ever seen. Protests in the United States against police brutality affirming that Black Lives Matter catalyze a global awakening to the realities of racialized oppression. Information technologies ensuring that news from every country reverberates around the world in minutes carry blatant falsehoods about a "stolen" election from a sitting president of the United States, undermining global confidence in the American democratic process. And with more than 200 million migrants worldwide, migration and immigration are creating societies that are enormously diverse, both linguistically and culturally, and that are navigating uncharted waters toward fair and inclusive nationhood.

More than ever, people, cultures, and nations are interdependent, requiring young people who are capable and disposed to solve problems on a global scale and participate effectively in a global economic and civic environment. Put simply, schools must prepare students to investigate the world, recognize perspectives, communicate with diverse audiences, and take action.

In 2018, OECD included a two-part assessment of global competence in its triannual Programme of International Student Assessment (PISA). Students in 27 countries took the global competence cognitive test and completed a global competence module in the student questionnaire. Students in 39 other countries completed the global competence module in the questionnaire only. According to Andreas Schleicher (2020), "The most interesting finding from this new PISA assessment is that many school activities, including the organization of learning at school, contact with people from other cultures, and learning other languages, are positively associated with global competence." Following are some key findings from the assessment:

Students in countries ranking highest on the traditional PISA measures were often among those showing the highest levels of global competence, although with notable exceptions. For example, Colombia's students struggle on PISA reading, mathematics, and science tasks but were among the highest in global competence. This may be related to the efforts by this country torn by civil war to strengthen civic skills and connections across internal cultural gaps.

In many countries, students who engaged in higher levels of learning about the beliefs, norms, values, perspectives, and customs of diverse cultural groups tended to have more positive attitudes and dispositions toward other people and cultures. Global competence doesn't happen of its own accord; it depends on schools' concerted efforts to integrate global learning in both the curriculum and instructional activities.

Economically advantaged students have access to more opportunities to learn global and intercultural skills than disadvantaged students. The data also show that disadvantaged students tend to have less positive attitudes toward other people and cultures. Their relative lack of access to global learning is not because their schools lack access to such opportunities, but rather because within-school mechanisms steer disadvantaged students away from higher engagement in such activities.

Although principals indicated that teachers generally held positive multicultural beliefs, students perceived a level of discrimination by their teachers toward some groups, and those perceptions seem closely related to student attitudes. The PISA results show a consistent relationship between students' perception of discrimination in their school and lower levels of respect for people from other cultures, more negative attitudes toward immigrants, and less awareness of intercultural communication. Students who perceived discrimination by their teachers toward particular groups, such as immigrants, exhibited similar negative attitudes.

Teachers generally report being confident in their ability to teach diverse populations of students. At the same time, teachers report a high need for training in such areas as teaching in multicultural and multilingual settings, teaching intercultural communication, and teaching about equity and diversity.

Having contact with people from other countries at school and in one's family, neighborhood, and circle of friends is positively associated with students' intercultural skills and attitudes toward living with others. Contact with people of different origins and cultures can foster understanding and mitigate prejudice. This finding further implies that schools and school systems that do not have diverse populations will need to make special efforts to ensure their students benefit from culture exposure.

Inequities were found between boys and girls in access to opportunities to develop global competence. Boys, for example, were more often expected to express and discuss their personal opinions on world events and analyze global issues. In contrast, girls were more often expected to learn how to solve conflicts and understand different cultural perspectives on global issues. These data suggest that boys may be expected to develop a more "take charge" mindset, whereas girls are socialized to take a more collaborative approach to addressing difference.

In nearly all countries, students' ability to speak two or more languages was associated with positive attitudes toward people from backgrounds different from their own. More than 90 percent of all students surveyed reported that they learn at least one foreign language in school. The largest proportion of students (more than 60 percent) who reported they do *not* learn any foreign language in school were from the English-speaking nations of Australia, New Zealand, and Scotland.

What Stakeholders Can Do

Recognizing the key roles that both public and private sectors play in education, this concluding section focuses on what various stakeholders can do to further global competence. We hope that synergistic actions across sectors will take global competence from the margins to the mainstream of education and cultural policy in the United States and beyond.

What Teachers Can Do

- Target high-leverage entry points within the curriculum to engage students in rigorous global inquiry using national, local, and school expectations (for example, state standards) as gateways to deep learning and intellectual development.

- Create professional learning communities that infuse the curriculum with opportunities for students to investigate and analyze issues of global significance, communicate findings to diverse audiences, and improve conditions locally and globally.

- Connect your classroom and curriculum to cultural and educational institutions that offer additional opportunities for students to hone their global competence. Institutions may include museums; civic institutions (Red Cross, Rotary/Kiwanis/Lions); after-school and extended-learning programs (YMCA/YWCA, Boys and Girls Clubs); and nongovernmental organizations that promote global competence and intercultural communication (Bridges to Understanding, Taking IT Global, World Savvy, iEARN). Such authentic audiences can give students invaluable feedback on their global projects.

- Develop your own global competence by taking advantage of opportunities to learn about the world's cultures, languages, and interdependent systems, and broaden your perspective through travel and study abroad. The Fulbright Teachers for Global Classrooms Program (www.fulbrightteacherexchanges.org/programs/tgc) and Fulbright Distinguished Awards in Teaching (www.fulbrightteacherexchanges.org/programs/da) offer a range of international professional development opportunities to teachers.

What School Leaders Can Do

- Lead your education communities in developing a deep understanding of the importance of global competence for the success of every student and in considering what a school's mission should be in the 21st century. Highlight how developing global competence is essential to combat racial, ethnic, and religious prejudice and promote equity.

- Identify opportunities for your schools to investigate how addressing matters of global significance can become a mainstay of a school's culture, reflected in its structures, practices, and relationships with people and institutions outside the school.

- Pilot new and strengthen existing approaches to promote global competence, from new course offerings in world languages and other internationally focused content, to globally focused service learning and internships, to international travel and virtual exchange opportunities for students and teachers. Career and technical education (CTE) programs are an often-overlooked opportunity; global competence aligns to all CTE career pathways and is vital to prepare students for work in the global economy.

- Identify and promote best practices in global education stemming from your schools and communities. Create conditions for interested stakeholders (teachers, administrators, parents, and businesses) to reflect on the opportunities embedded in best practices and to consider what they can do to expand their reach.

What District Leaders Can Do

- Review existing policies, programs, and funding priorities to see whether they promote the development of global competence among all populations served by the schools.

- Recruit, develop, and sustain personnel and policy review committees that want to promote global understanding and global perspectives in teaching.

- Require students to demonstrate and develop global competence through authentic performances and other valid and equitable measures of learning.

What State and Federal Policymakers Can Do

- At the state and federal levels, appoint a cross-departmental committee with authority to coordinate a governmentwide approach to prioritizing activities that promote global competence activities.

- Increase funding and incentives to further develop programs in world languages (including indigenous languages and cultures) and global education in states and K–12 districts, prioritizing underserved youth and elementary and middle school students.

- Embed global competence–focused professional learning and resource development into weighted scoring formulas for existing and new grant programs managed by state education departments and the U.S. Department of Education.

- Increase support for the U.S. Department of Education's Title VI grant programs, and encourage more partnerships among K–12 systems and programs supporting centers with outreach functions.

- Participate in future OECD international assessments of global competence and develop partnerships with OECD, UNESCO, AFS Intercultural Programs, and other international organizations to promote and assess students' global competence.

- Increase support for the U.S. Department of State's Bureau of Educational and Cultural Affairs.

What Colleges and Universities Can Do

- Recognize the value of global competence certifications and experiences in your admissions processes.

- Prepare globally competent graduates who understand the world and who are ready to participate critically and creatively in it through their chosen fields of work and study.

- Retool teacher preparation programs to integrate international learning opportunities, and substantially strengthen requirements and support for developing the capacity among prospective teachers to teach for global competence.

- Encourage scholarly research and program evaluation to deepen understanding of the demands and opportunities of global competence education. Such work may range from revealing basic socio-cognitive processes involved in the development of global competence; to measuring the effect of diverse approaches to integrating global competence in K–12 curriculum, assessment, and instruction; to examining the role of global competence education in school improvement; to transforming poor-performing schools; to taking well-functioning schools from "good to great."

- Prioritize the development of global competence as part of the mission and institutional practice of higher education to ensure that learning how to investigate, communicate, and act within a global economy and interdependent world becomes an essential element of what it means to be a well-educated person in the 21st century.

Going Global—It's the Only Way to Go

Our discussion of global competence in this book—its rationale, definition, and manifestation in educational practice and policy—should serve as both inspiration and practical guidance for all those who seek to prepare students to engage the world. The variety of student work that we have examined here, along with the experiences of teachers from across the world, show that teaching and learning for global competence are within the reach of every type of school. We hope you will use these ideas—and incorporate your own—to ensure that every student is well prepared for the challenges and opportunities of an interdependent, global environment.

Appendix:
Global Competence Matrices

Global Competence Matrix. 143

Global Competence Matrix for the Arts 144

Global Competence Matrix for English Language Arts. 146

Global Competence Matrix for Mathematics 147

Global Competence Matrix for Science. 149

Global Competence Matrix for Social Studies 151

Global Competence Matrix for World Languages 152

Global Competence Matrix

Investigate the World	Recognize Perspectives	Communicate Ideas	Take Action
Students investigate the world beyond their immediate environment.	Students recognize their own and others' perspectives.	Students communicate their ideas effectively with diverse audiences.	Students translate their ideas and findings into appropriate actions to improve conditions.
Students			
Identify an issue, generate a question, and explain the significance of locally, regionally, or globally focused researchable questions.	Recognize and express their own perspective on situations, events, issues, or phenomena and identify the influences on that perspective.	Recognize and express how diverse audiences may perceive different meanings from the same information and how that affects communication.	Identify and create opportunities for personal or collaborative action to address situations, events, issues, or phenomena in ways that improve conditions.
Use a variety of languages and domestic and international sources and media to identify and weigh relevant evidence to address a globally significant researchable question.	Examine perspectives of other people, groups, or schools of thought and identify the influences on those perspectives.	Listen to and communicate effectively with diverse people, using appropriate verbal and non-verbal behavior, languages, and strategies.	Assess options and plan actions based on evidence and the potential for impact, taking into account previous approaches, varied perspectives, and potential consequences.
Analyze, integrate, and synthesize evidence collected to construct coherent responses to globally significant researchable questions.	Explain how cultural interactions influence situations, events, issues, or phenomena, including the development of knowledge.	Select and use appropriate technology and media to communicate with diverse audiences.	Act, personally or collaboratively, in creative and ethical ways to contribute to improvement locally, regionally, or globally and assess the effect of the actions taken.

(continued)

Global Competence Matrix—(*continued*)

Develop an argument based on compelling evidence that considers multiple perspectives and draws defensible conclusions.	Articulate how differential access to knowledge, technology, and resources affects quality of life and perspectives.	Reflect on how effective communication affects understanding and collaboration in an interdependent world.	Reflect on their capacity to advocate for and contribute to improvement locally, regionally, or globally.

Global Competence Matrix for the Arts

Investigate the World	Recognize Perspectives	Communicate Ideas	Take Action
Students use the arts to investigate the world beyond their immediate environment.	Students use the arts to recognize their own and others' perspectives.	Students communicate their ideas effectively with diverse audiences using art.	Students use the arts to translate their ideas and findings into appropriate actions to improve conditions.
Students			
Identify themes or issues and frame researchable questions of local, regional, or global significance that call for or emerge from investigations in the arts.	Recognize and express their own artistic perspectives and sensibilities and determine how those are influenced by their background and experience in the world, and, conversely, how their perspectives and sensibilities about the world are influenced by their experience in the arts.	Examine how diverse audiences may interpret and react to artistic expressions differently.	Identify existing and innovative opportunities to use the arts, personally and collaboratively, to contribute to improvements locally, regionally, or globally.

Identify, observe, and interpret a variety of domestic and international works of visual or performing art, materials, and ideas and determine their relevance to globally significant themes.	Examine how the artistic perspectives and sensibilities of different individuals, groups, and schools of thought are influenced by their experience in the world and, conversely, how their views of the world are influenced by their experience in the arts.	Appreciate a variety of artistic expressions and use artistic repertoires, forms, or media to communicate with diverse audiences around the world.	Assess options for the use of the arts and plan actions considering available evidence, previous approaches, and potential consequences.
Analyze, integrate, and synthesize insights to envision and create an artistic expression of globally significant themes and submit this expression for critique.	Explain how cultural interaction influences the development of artistic products, ideas, concepts, knowledge, and aesthetics.	Select and use appropriate technologies to enhance the effectiveness and reach of a work of art.	Use the arts to act, both personally and collaboratively, in creative and ethical ways to contribute to improvements locally, regionally, or globally and reflect on the effect of the actions taken.
Engage in critical conversations based on compelling evidence and consider multiple perspectives to draw defensible conclusions about the effectiveness of a work of art to illuminate globally significant themes.	Explore and describe how, despite differential access to knowledge, technology, and resources, individuals and groups produce meaningful art that enables human expression and connection around the world.	Reflect on how the arts affect understanding and collaboration in an interdependent world.	Reflect on their capacity to advocate for and contribute to improvements locally, regionally, or globally through the arts.

Global Competence Matrix for English Language Arts

Investigate the World	Recognize Perspectives	Communicate Ideas	Take Action
Students use English language arts to investigate the world beyond their immediate environment.	Students use English language arts to recognize their own and others' perspectives.	Students communicate their ideas effectively with diverse audiences using English language arts.	Students use English language arts to translate their ideas and findings into appropriate actions to improve conditions.
Students			
Explore a range of domestic and international texts and media to identify and frame researchable questions of local, regional, or global significance.	Recognize and express their own perspectives on situations, events, issues, or phenomena and determine how that perspective has developed or changed based on exposure to a variety of texts and media from different periods and cultures.	Recognize and express how diverse audiences may perceive different meanings from the same texts or media and how those different perspectives affect communication and collaboration.	Identify and create opportunities for personal and collaborative actions, using reading, writing, speaking, and listening to address situations, events, and issues to improve conditions.
Use a variety of domestic and international sources, media, and languages to identify and weigh relevant evidence to address globally significant researchable questions.	Examine perspectives of other people, groups, or schools of thought within and about texts and media from around the world and identify the influences on those perspectives.	Use appropriate language, behavior, language arts strategies (reading, writing, listening, and speaking), and nonverbal strategies to effectively communicate with diverse audiences.	Assess options and plan action based on evidence from text and media and the potential for impact, taking into account previous approaches, varied perspectives, and potential consequences.

Analyze, integrate, synthesize, and appropriately cite sources of evidence collected to construct coherent responses to globally significant researchable questions.	Explain how cultural interactions within and around texts or media are important to the situations, events, issues, or themes that are depicted and to readers' understandings of those texts and media.	Select and use appropriate technology, media, and literary genres to share insights, findings, concepts, and proposals with diverse audiences.	Use language arts skills to act, personally and collaboratively, in creative and ethical ways to contribute to sustainable improvement and assess the effect of the action.
Develop and logically and persuasively present an argument based on compelling evidence that considers multiple perspectives and draws defensible conclusions about a globally significant issue.	Explore and describe how differential access to literacy and to a range of works from different genres, periods, and places affects perspectives and quality of life.	Reflect on how effective communication in various genres affects understanding and collaboration in an interdependent world.	Reflect on how effective reading, writing, listening, and speaking contribute to their capacity to advocate for and contribute to improvement locally, regionally, or globally.

Global Competence Matrix for Mathematics

Investigate the World	Recognize Perspectives	Communicate Ideas	Take Action
Students use mathematics to investigate the world beyond their immediate environment.	Students recognize their own and others' perspectives through the study of mathematics.	Students communicate their ideas about mathematics effectively with diverse audiences.	Students use their mathematical knowledge and skills to translate their ideas and findings into appropriate actions to improve conditions.

(continued)

Global Competence Matrix for Mathematics—(*continued*)

Students			
Identify issues and frame researchable questions of local, regional, or global significance that call for or emerge from a mathematical or statistical approach.	Recognize and express their own perspective and understanding of the world and determine how mathematics and statistics influence and enhance that perspective and understanding.	Recognize and express how diverse audiences may perceive different meanings from the same mathematical or statistical information and how that affects communication and collaboration.	Identify and create opportunities to use mathematical or statistical analyses to enable personal or collaborative action that improves conditions.
Select or construct appropriate mathematical or statistical models or approaches to address globally significant researchable questions.	Examine how the perspectives of other people, groups, or schools of thought influence the ways mathematical and statistical findings are interpreted and applied and, conversely, how an understanding of and access to mathematics and statistics influence those perspectives.	Use appropriate language, behavior, and mathematical and statistical representations to effectively communicate with diverse audiences.	Use mathematical or statistical descriptions, representations, or models to plan, weigh, and defend plausible and ethical actions for addressing a globally significant issue, taking into account previous approaches, varied perspectives, and potential consequences.
Conduct, assess, and synthesize mathematical or statistical analyses to develop or review evidence, draw conclusions, and make decisions concerning globally significant questions.	Explain how the development of mathematical knowledge is based on the contributions of different cultures and influenced by cultural interactions and, conversely, how societies and cultures are influenced by mathematics.	Select and use appropriate technology and media to model, analyze, represent, and communicate mathematical ideas for diverse audiences and purposes.	Use mathematics and statistics to support personal or collaborative ethical and creative action that contributes to sustainable improvement and assess the effect of the action.

Interpret and apply the results of mathematical or statistical analyses to develop and defend an argument about a globally significant issue.	Explore and describe how differential access to mathematical and statistical knowledge, technology, and resources affects both the perspectives and quality of life of individuals and society.	Reflect on how mathematics contributes to cross-cultural communication and collaboration in an interdependent world.	Reflect on how mathematics and statistics contribute to their capacity to advocate for local, regional, or global improvement.

Global Competence Matrix for Science

Investigate the World	Recognize Perspectives	Communicate Ideas	Take Action
Students use science to investigate the world beyond their immediate environment.	Students recognize their own and others' perspectives through the study of science.	Students communicate their ideas about science effectively with diverse audiences.	Students use their scientific knowledge and skills to translate their ideas and findings into appropriate actions that improve conditions.
Students			
Identify issues and frame investigable questions of local, regional, or global significance that call for a scientific approach or emerge from science.	Recognize and express their own perspective on situations, events, issues, or phenomena and determine how that perspective, along with their entire understanding of the world, is influenced by science.	Recognize and express how diverse audiences may interpret differently or make different assumptions about the same scientific information and how that affects communication and collaboration.	Identify and create opportunities in which scientific analysis or inquiry can enable personal or collaborative action to improve conditions.

(continued)

Global Competence Matrix for Science—(*continued*)

Use a variety of domestic and international sources to identify and weigh relevant scientific evidence to address globally significant researchable questions.	Examine scientific ways of knowing and perspectives about science of other people, groups, and schools of thought and identify the influences on those perspectives.	Use varying scientific practices, behaviors, and strategies to verbally and nonverbally communicate scientific information effectively with diverse audiences, including the international scientific community.	Assess options, plan actions, and design solutions based on scientific evidence and the potential for impact, taking into account previous approaches, varied perspectives, and potential consequences.
Design and conduct a scientific inquiry to collect and analyze data, construct plausible and coherent conclusions, or raise questions for further globally significant study.	Explain how cultural interactions influence the development of scientific knowledge.	Select and use appropriate technology and media to communicate about science and share data with experts and peers around the world.	Act, personally or collaboratively, in creative and ethical ways to implement scientifically-based solutions that contribute to sustainable improvements and assess the effect of the action.
Interpret and apply the results of a scientific inquiry to develop and defend an argument that considers multiple perspectives about a globally significant issue.	Explore and describe the consequences of differential access to scientific knowledge and to the potential benefits of that knowledge.	Reflect on how effective communication affects scientific understanding and international collaboration in an interdependent world.	Reflect on how scientific knowledge and skills contribute to their capacity to advocate for improvement locally, regionally, or globally.

Global Competence Matrix for Social Studies

Investigate the World	Recognize Perspectives	Communicate Ideas	Take Action
Students use social studies to investigate the world beyond their immediate environment.	Students use social studies to recognize their own and others' perspectives.	Students communicate their ideas about social studies effectively with diverse audiences.	Students use social studies to translate their ideas and findings into appropriate actions to improve conditions.
Students			
Identify issues and frame researchable questions of local, regional, or global significance that call for or emerge from investigations in the social sciences.	Recognize and express their own perspective on situations, events, issues, or phenomena and identify the cultural, social, economic, political, geographical, and historical influences that inform that perspective.	Recognize and express how diverse audiences may interpret and use the same information in different ways and for different purposes and how that affects communication and collaboration.	Identify and create opportunities for personal and collaborative action and civic engagement to contribute to sustainable improvements and quality of life.
Identify and weigh relevant evidence from primary and secondary documents, using a variety of domestic and international sources, media, and languages, to address globally significant researchable questions.	Examine the role of place, time, culture, society, and resources in the perspectives held by people, groups, or schools of thought.	Use the language of social scientists and adapt their modes of communication and behavior to interact effectively with diverse audiences.	Assess options, plan actions, and engage in civil discourse, considering previous approaches, varied perspectives, political viability, and potential consequences.

(continued)

Global Competence Matrix for Social Studies—(*continued*)

Analyze, integrate, and synthesize evidence using knowledge, methods, and critical skills in the social sciences to deepen their understanding of, and construct coherent responses to, globally significant issues.	Explain how individuals, societies, events, and the development of knowledge are influenced by the movement and interaction of ideas, goods, capital, and people.	Select and use technology and media strategically to create products, express views, and communicate and collaborate with people of diverse backgrounds.	Act, personally and collaboratively, in ways that are creative, ethical, and informed by the knowledge and methods of the social sciences to contribute to sustainable improvement and assess the effect of the action.
Produce an account based on compelling social scientific evidence and multiple perspectives that exhibits understanding of a global issue and that raises new questions or advocates for action.	Explore and describe how geopolitical differences, as well as access to knowledge, resources, and technology, affect the options, choices, and quality of life of people around the world.	Reflect on how communication contributes to or impedes understanding, collaboration, negotiation, and diplomacy in an interdependent world.	Reflect on their capacity to draw on the social sciences to advocate for and contribute to improvement locally, regionally, or globally.

Global Competence Matrix for World Languages

Investigate the World	Recognize Perspectives	Communicate Ideas	Take Action
Students use world languages to investigate the world beyond their immediate environment.	Students recognize their own and others' perspectives through the study of world languages.	Students communicate their ideas effectively with diverse audiences using world languages.	Students use world languages to translate their ideas and findings into appropriate actions to improve conditions.

Students			
Use knowledge of language and culture to identify issues and frame researchable questions of local, regional, or global significance.	Recognize and express their own perspectives and understandings of the world and determine how language and culture inform and shape those perspectives and understandings.	Recognize and express how linguistically diverse people may perceive different meanings from the same words or nonverbal cues and how this affects communication and collaboration.	Use their native and studied languages and culture to identify and create opportunities for personal or collaborative action to improve conditions.
Use a variety of domestic and international sources, media, and experiences in the target language to identify and weigh relevant evidence to address globally significant researchable questions.	Examine the perspectives of other people, groups, or schools of thought and how language and culture influence those perspectives.	Use the target language for interpersonal, interpretive, and presentational purposes, including appropriate verbal and nonverbal behavior and strategies, to communicate with the target culture.	Use linguistic and cultural knowledge to assess options and plan actions, taking into account previous approaches, varied perspectives, and potential consequences.
Analyze, integrate, and synthesize evidence, taking into account cultural and linguistic contexts, to construct coherent responses appropriate to globally significant questions.	Explain how cultural and linguistic interactions influence situations, events, issues, ideas, and language, including the development of knowledge.	Select and use appropriate technology and media to connect with native speakers of the target language; present information, concepts, or ideas of global significance; or develop creative products within the target language.	Use their native and studied languages and cross-cultural knowledge to act, personally and collaboratively, in creative and ethical ways to contribute to sustainable improvement and assess the effect of the action.

(continued)

Global Competence Matrix for World Languages—*(continued)*

Use their knowledge of language and culture to develop an argument based on compelling evidence that considers multiple perspectives and draws defensible conclusions about a globally significant issue.	Explore and describe how different levels of language proficiency and access to knowledge, technology, and resources affect opportunities and quality of life for individuals and societies.	Reflect on how the use and knowledge of diverse languages promote effective communication, understanding, and collaboration with and within various cultures.	Reflect on how proficiency in more than one language contributes to their capacity to advocate for and contribute to improvement locally, regionally, or globally.

Source: From *Educating for Global Competence: Preparing Our Youth to Engage the World* (pp. 102–108), by V. Boix Mansilla and A. Jackson, 2011, Council of Chief State School Officers & Asia Society Partnership for Global Learning. Copyright 2011 by the Council of Chief State School Officers. Reprinted with permission.

References

Allen, D. (2016). Toward a connected society. In E. Lewis & N. Cantor (Eds.), *Our compelling interests: The value of diversity for democracy and a prosperous society* (pp. 71–105). Princeton University Press.

Allen, D. (2019). Are you a changemaker? Youth Participatory Politics Research Network, Harvard University. https://yppactionframe.fas.harvard.edu/home

Allen, D., & Light, J. S. (2015). *From voice to influence: Understanding citizenship in a digital age*. University of Chicago Press.

American Councils for International Education. (2017). *The national K–12 foreign language enrollment survey report*. https://www.americancouncils.org/sites/default/files/FLE-report-June17.pdf

Appiah, K. A. (2008). Education for global citizenship. In the National Society for the Study of Education (Ed.), *Yearbook of the National Society for the Study of Education* (pp. 83–99). University of Chicago Press.

Asia Society (n.d.). Profile of an International Studies Schools Network (ISSN) high school graduate. www.asiasociety.org/education

Asia Society. (2008). *Going global: Preparing our students for an interconnected world.* https://asiasociety.org/education/going-global

Asia Society & Longview Foundation. (2016). *Preparing a globally competent workforce through high-quality career and technical education.* https://asiasociety.org/sites/default/files/preparing-a-globally-competent-work-force-june-2016.pdf

Asia Society & OECD. (2018). *Teaching for global competence in a rapidly changing world.* https://asiasociety.org/education/teaching-global-competence-rapidly-changing-world

Bennet, M. (2009). Defining, measuring, and facilitating intercultural learning: A conceptual introduction to the *Intercultural Education* double supplement. *Intercultural Education, 20*, 1–2.

Boix Mansilla, V. (2016). How to be a global thinker. *Educational Leadership, 74*(4), 10–16.

Boix Mansilla, V. (2017). *Global thinking: An ID-global bundle to foster global thinking dispositions through global thinking routines.* Project Zero, Harvard Graduate School of Education. http://www.pz.harvard.edu/resources/global-thinking

Boix Mansilla, V. (2018). *Re-imagining migration: Toward a new educational framework for a world on the move.* Project Zero, Harvard Graduate School of Education. www.pz.harvard.edu/projects/re-imagining-migration

Boix Mansilla, V., & Chua, F. (2017). *Signature pedagogies in global competence education: Understanding quality teaching practice.* In S. Choo, D. Sawch, A. Villanueva, & R. Vinz (Eds.), *Educating for the 21st century* (pp. 93–115*).* Springer.

Boix Mansilla, V., Chua, F., & Dawes, E. (2010). *The world studies extended essay nurturing global consciousness and interdisciplinary inquiry: Teachers' guide.* International Baccalaureate Press.

Boix Mansilla, V., & Gardner, H. (1998). What are the qualities of understanding? In M. S. Wiske (Ed.), *Teaching for understanding: Linking research with practice* (pp. 161–196). Jossey-Bass.

Boix Mansilla, V., & Gardner, H. (2006). From teaching globalization to teaching for global consciousness. In M. Suárez-Orozco (Ed.), *Globalization and learning* (pp. 47–66). Jossey-Bass.

Boix Mansilla, V., & Jackson, A. (2011). *Educating for global competence: Preparing our youth to engage the world.* Council of Chief State School Officers & Asia Society Partnership for Global Learning.

Boix Mansilla, V., Miller, C. M., & Gardner, H. (2000). On disciplinary lenses and interdisciplinary work. In S. Wineburg & P. Grossman (Eds.), *Interdisciplinary curriculum: Challenges to implementation.* Teachers College Press.

Boix Mansilla, V., & Schleicher, A. (2022). *Big picture thinking: How to educate the whole person for an interconnected world: Principles and practices.* OECD. https://issuu.com/oecd.publishing/docs/big-picture-thinking-educating-global-competence

Boix Mansilla, V., & Wilson, D. (2020). What is global competence, and what might it look like in Chinese schools? *Journal of Research in International Education, 19*(1), 3–22.

Breakstone, J., Smith, M., Wineburg, S., Rapaport, A., Carle, J., Garland, M., & Saavedra, A. (2019). *Students' civic online reasoning: A national portrait.* Stanford Graduate School of Education. https://purl.stanford.edu/gf151tb4868

Bringle, R. G., & Clayton, P. H. (2012). Civic education through service-learning: What, how, and why? In L. McIlrath, A. Lyons, & R. Munck (Eds.), *Higher education and civic engagement: Comparative perspectives* (pp. 101–124). Palgrave.

British Council. (2013). *Culture at work: The value of intercultural skills in the workplace.*

Bruner, J. S. (1960). *The process of education.* Harvard University Press.

Center for Global Education. (n.d.). SAGE advice. https://asiasociety.org/education/sage-advice

Coatsworth, J. H. (2004). Globalization, growth, and welfare in history. In M. Suárez-Orozco & D. Qin-Hilliard (Eds.), *Globalization: Culture and education in the new millennium* (pp. 38–55). University of California Press.

Common Core State Standards Initiative. (2009). English language arts standards. www.corestandards.org/ELA-Literacy

Council of Europe. (2016). *Competences for a democratic culture: Living together as equals in culturally diverse democratic societies.* https://rm.coe.int/16806ccc07

Crawford, E., Higgins, H., & Hilburn, J. (2020). Using a global competence model in an instructional design course before social studies methods: A developmental approach to global teacher education. *Journal of Social Study Research, 44*(4), 367–381.

Deardorff, D. K. (Ed.). (2009). *The Sage handbook of intercultural competence.* Sage.

Deardorff, D. K. (2013). *Promoting understanding and development of intercultural dialogue and peace: A comparative analysis and global perspective of regional studies on intercultural competence.* UNESCO Division of Cultural Policies and Intercultural Dialogue.

Deardorff, D. K. (2020). *Manual for developing intercultural competences: Story circles.* UNESCO; Routledge. https://unesdoc.unesco.org/ark:/48223/pf0000370336

Deardorff, D. K., & Bowman, K. (2011). *Beneath the tip of the iceberg: Improving English and understanding U.S. cultural patterns.* University of Michigan Press.

Denver Center for International Studies. (n.d.). Core values and leadership domains. https://dcis.dpsk12.org/about/core-values-leadership-domains/

Du Bois, W. E. B. (2007). *The souls of Black folk.* Oxford University Press.

Fischman W., Solomon, B., Greenspan, D., & Gardner, H. (2004). *Making good: How young people cope with moral dilemmas at work.* Harvard University Press.

Gardner, H. (2009). *Five minds for the future.* Harvard Business School Press.

Gardner, H., & Davis, A. (2013). *The app generation: How today's youth navigate identity, intimacy, and imagination in a digital world.* Yale University Press.

Global Education Certificate. (2021). What is a global education certificate? http://globaledcertificate.org/about/

Google. (2019). Smart, alert, strong, kind, brave. Be Internet Awesome: Digital Citizenship Safety Curriculum. https://storage.googleapis.com/gweb-interland.appspot.com/en-us/hub/pdfs/Google_BeInternetAwesome_DigitalCitizenshipSafety_2019Curriculum.pdf

Grotzer, T. (2012*). Learning causality in a complex world: Understandings of consequence.* Rowman & Littlefield Education.

Harari, Y. (2018). *21 lessons for the 21st century* (1st ed.). Spiegel & Grau.

Haste, H. (2007). Good thinking: The creative and competent mind. In A. Craft, H. Gardner, & G. Claxton (Eds.), *Creativity, wisdom, and trusteeship* (pp. 96–104*).* Corwin.

Heath, S. B. (1983). *Ways with words: Language, life, and work in communities and classrooms.* McGraw-Hill.

Ito, M., Gutiérrez, K., Livingstone, S., Penuel, B., Rhodes, J., Salen, K., Schor, J., Sefton-Green, J., & Watkins, S. C. (2013). *Connected learning: An agenda for research and design.* Digital Media and Learning Research Hub.

Jackson, A. (2020). Getting clearer: Dismantling systemic oppression in public education: Lessons from Toronto and Ontario. *Getting Smart.* https://www.gettingsmart.com/2020/04/getting-clearer-dismantling-systemic-oppression-in-public-education/

James, C. (2014). *Disconnected: Youth, new media, and the ethics gap.* MIT Media Press.

Kahne, J., Middaugh, E., & Allen, D. (2015). Youth, new media, and the rise of participatory politics. In E. Lewis & N. Cantor (Eds.), *From voice to influence: Understanding citizenship in a digital age* (pp. 35–58). University of Chicago Press.

Klein, J. D. (2013). Making meaning in a standards-based world: Negotiating tensions in global education. *Educational Forum, 77*(4), 481–490.

Kuhn, D. (2008). *Education for thinking.* Harvard University Press.

Kymlicka, W. (1995). *Multicultural citizenship: A liberal theory of minority rights.* Oxford University Press.

Levitt, P., & Lamba, D. (2009). *It's not just about the economy, stupid: Social remittances revisited.* Migration Information Source. https://www.migrationpolicy.org/article/its-not-just-about-economy-stupid-social-remittances-revisited

Levy, F., & Murnane, R. (2004). *The new division of labor: How computers are creating the next job market.* Russell Sage.

Longview Foundation. (n.d.-a). International education planning rubric: State strategies to prepare globally competent students. https://asiasociety.org/files/statesrubric.pdf

Longview Foundation. (n.d.-b). Internationalizing teacher preparation. https://longviewfdn.org/index.php/programs/internationalizing-teacher-prep/

Longview Foundation. (n.d.-c). State and district network for international education. https://longviewfdn.org/programs/state-network-intl-education/

Louv, R. (2011). *The nature principle: Human restoration and the end of nature-deficit disorder.* Algonquin Books.

Manyika, J., Lund, S., Auguste, B., & Ramaswamy, S. (2012, March 1). *Help wanted: The future of work in advanced economies.* McKinsey Global Institute. https://www.mckinsey.com/featured-insights/employment-and-growth/future-of-work-in-advanced-economies

Massachusetts Department of Education. (2006). Massachusetts science and technology/engineering curriculum framework. https://www.doe.mass.edu/frameworks/archive.html

McAuliffe, M., & Triandafyllidou, A. (Eds.). (2021.) *World migration report 2022.* International Organization for Migration (IOM). https://publications.iom.int/books/world-migration-report-2022

Mulgrave School. (n.d.). Our mission & values. https://www.mulgrave.com/about-us/our-mission-values

National Assessment of Educational Progress (NAEP). (2019). *The nation's report card.* https://www.nationsreportcard.gov/

National Center on Education and the Economy. (2008). *Tough choices or tough times: The report of the new commission on the skills of the American workforce, revised and expanded.* Jossey-Bass.

National Geographic Society. (2020). GeoChallenge. https://www.nationalgeographic.org/education/student-experiences/geochallenge

National Governors' Association Center for Best Practices & Council of Chief State School Officers. (2010). *Common core state standards.*

National Research Council. (2010). *Adapting to the impacts of climate change.* Report in brief. National Academies Press. https://nap.nationalacademies.org/resource/12783/Adapting_Report_Brief_final.pdf

OECD. (2018). *Preparing our youth for an inclusive and sustainable world: The OECD PISA global competence framework.* https://www.oecd.org/pisa/Handbook-PISA-2018-Global-Competence.pdf

OECD. (2019). Students' socio-economic status and performance. In *PISA 2018 results (Vol. II): Where all students can succeed.* https://www.oecd-ilibrary .org/education/pisa-2018-results-volume-ii_f7986824-en

OECD. (2020). 2018 PISA global competence. https://www.oecd.org/pisa/ pisa-2018-global-competence.htm

Pacheco, R., Frodeman, R., & Klein, J. (2017). *The Oxford handbook of interdisciplinarity* (2nd ed.). Oxford University Press.

Parham, A., & Allen, D. (2015). Achieving rooted cosmopolitanism in the digital age. In D. Allen & J. S. Light (Eds.), *From voice to influence: Understanding citizenship in a digital age.* University of Chicago Press.

Perkins, D. (1992). *Smart schools: Better thinking and learning for every child.* Free Press.

Perkins, D. N. (2009). *Making learning whole: How seven principles of teaching can transform education.* Jossey-Bass.

Perkins, D. N. (2014). *Futurewise: Educating our children for a changing world.* Jossey-Bass.

Perkins, D. N., Tishman, S., Ritchhart, R., Donis, K., & Andrade, A. (2000). Intelligence in the wild: A dispositional view of educational traits. *Educational Psychology Review, 12*(3), 269–293.

Pew Hispanic Center. (2013). *A nation of immigrants: A portrait of the 40 million, including 11 million unauthorized.* Pew Research Center.

Pew Research Center. (2016). *The state of American jobs.* https://www.pewsocialtrends.org/2016/10/06/1-changes-in-the-american-workplace/

Re-imagining Migration. (2021). Our approach. https://reimaginingmigration. org/educating-immigrant-youth/

Reimers, F. (2020). *Educating students to improve the world.* Springer Briefs in Education. Springer.

Rideout, V., Peebles, A., Mann, S., & Robb, M. B. (2022). *Common Sense census: Media use by tweens and teens, 2021.* Common Sense. https://www.common-sensemedia.org/research/the-common-sense-census-media-use-by-tweens-and-teens-2021

Rogers, J., Ishimoto, M., Kwako, A., Berryman, A., & Diera, C. (2019). *School and society in the age of Trump.* UCLA's Institute for Democracy, Education, and Access.

Sachs, J. (2008). *Common wealth: Economics for a crowded planet.* Penguin.

Satrapi, M. (2003). *Persepolis.* Pantheon.

Schleicher, A. (2019). *PISA 2018 insights and interpretations.* PISA Publishing. www.oecd.org/pisa/PISA%202018%20Insights%20and%20Interpretations%20FINAL%20PDF.pdf

Schleicher, A. (2020, October 22). Are students ready to thrive in an interconnected world? The first PISA assessment of global competence provides some answers. https://oecdedutoday.com/students-ready-thrive-interconnected-world-first-pisa-assessment-global-competence/

Seelye, H. N. (1996). *Experiential activities for intercultural learning.* Intercultural Press.

Singapore Ministry of Education. (2021). 21st century competencies. https:// www.moe.gov.sg/education-in-sg/21st-century-competencies

Stevens Initiative. (2020). Curated resources: Stevens Initiative response to the Coronavirus pandemic. https://www.stevensinitiative.org/resource/curated-resources-stevens-initiative-response-to-the-coronavirus-pandemic/

Suarez, D. (2003). The development of empathetic dispositions through global experiences. *Educational Horizons, 81*(4), 180–182.

Suárez-Orozco, C., Suárez-Orozco, M. M., & Todorova, I. (2008). *Learning a new land: Immigrant students in American society.* Harvard University Press.

Suárez-Orozco, M. M. (2001). Globalization, immigration, and education: The research agenda. *Harvard Educational Review, 71*(3), 345–365.

Tichnor-Wagner, A., Parkhouse, H., Glazier, J., & Cain, J. M. (2019). *Becoming a globally competent teacher.* ASCD.

Toronto District School Board. (2017). *Enhancing equity task force: Report and recommendations.* https://www.tdsb.on.ca/Portals/0/community/docs/EET-FReportPdfVersion.pdf

Turkle, S. (2011). *Alone together: Why we expect more from technology and less from each other.* Basic Books.

UNESCO. (2007). *Guidelines on intercultural education.* https://unesdoc.unesco.org/ark:/48223/pf0000147878

UNESCO. (2013). *Intercultural competences: Conceptual and operational framework.* https://unesdoc.unesco.org/ark:/48223/pf0000219768

UNESCO. (2014). *Global citizenship education: Preparing learners for the challenges of the 21st century.* https://en.unesco.org/news/global-citizenship-education-preparing-learners-challenges-twenty-first-century-0

UNESCO. (2017). *Education for people and planet: Creating sustainable futures for all.* Global Education Monitoring report.

United Nations. (2019). International migrant stock 2019. Department of Economic and Social Affairs, Population Division. https://www.un.org/en/development/desa/population/migration/data/estimates2/estimates19.asp

United Nations. (2020a). Make the SDGs a reality. https://sdgs.un.org/

United Nations. (2020b). Sustainable development goals four: Ensure inclusive and equitable quality education and promote lifelong learning opportunities for all. https://sustainabledevelopment.un.org/sdg4

U.S. Department of Education. (2018). *Succeeding globally through international education and engagement.* https://sites.ed.gov/international/files/2018/11/Succeeding-Globally-Through-International-Education-and-Engagement-Update-2018.pdf

USA for UNHCR. (2022). Refugee statistics. https://www.unrefugees.org/refugee-facts/statistics/

Waters, M. (2007). *The new Americans: A guide to immigration since 1965.* Harvard University Press Reference Library.

Wiske, S. (1999). *Teaching for understanding: A practical framework.* Jossey-Bass.

Zaki, J. (2019). *The war for kindness: Building empathy in a fractured world.* Penguin Random House.

Zuckerman, E. (2013). *Rewire: Digital cosmopolitans in the age of connection.* Norton.

Index

The letter *f* following a page locator denotes a figure.

Ancient Number Systems lesson, 42–44
Arts, Global Competence Matrix for
  the, 144–145
assessment
  Earth Science Class, 97–100
  Global School Design Blueprint,
    106–107, 116
  PISA global competence cognitive
    test, 135–137

climate change, 13–16
Common Core State Standards, 32
communicating across differences
  dimension of global competence
    characteristics of, 64–66
    cognitive developmental progres-
      sions, 72*f*
    examples, 13, 20
    introduction, 26–27
    lesson examples, 66–70
    online, 65
    opportunities and challenges,
      70–72
conceptual age, 19–20
connectivity, digital global, 11,
  16–18
consciousness, double, 11–12
COVID-19 pandemic, 1–2, 7, 9
cultural exchange, digital, 18

cultural learning domain, 29
culture in the Global School Design
  Blueprint, 106, 108–109
cultures, interacting across. *See*
  communicating across differences
  dimension of global competence
curriculum, Global School Design Blueprint, 106–107, 111–114

democracy, 21
depth component, in essential learning, 30–31
development, sustainable. *See* taking
  action toward collective well-being
  and sustainable development dimension of global competence
Dewey, John, 3–4
digital citizens, preparing, 16–18
digital global connectivity, 16–18
digital media, average use per student
  per day, 15
diversity, thriving in a world of, 13
dominance paradigm, 4

Earth Sciences lesson, 87–88, 91–93,
  96–101
economy
  global migration and the, 11
  new global, 18–21

education
  global competence, 10
  interdisciplinary, 31
  paradigmatic shifts in, 3–4
education systems, challenges for, 124–126
egalitarian paradigm, 4
empathy, 18
engagement, 28–29, 90, 95–96

English Language Arts, Global Competence Matrix for, 146–147
environmental stewardship, 13–16
environmental sustainability learning domain, 30
ethics, global competence, 5
Examining Laughter in the United States and Afghanistan lesson, 57–59
Exploring Shelters Across the World lesson, 54–57
Exposing the Plight of the Colonized lesson, 69–70

fake news, 16–17
Faxing a Letter to Washington, D.C. lesson, 33–34
feedback, 98, 99–100
Framework for 21st Century Competencies, Singapore, 125
frameworks, purpose of, 2
Freire, Paulo, 4

global competence. *See also specific dimensions of*
  advocating for through public policy, 124–133
  benchmarks for, 123–124
  certification in, 126, 128
  defined, 5
  dimensions of, 24*f*
  drive toward, 123
  importance of, 135
  OECD framework for, 9–10, 21–22, 23–24, 24*f*
  performances of, 94–97
  qualities of learning underlying, 28–32
  rationale for, 7
  stakeholders' role in furthering, 137–141
  vision for, 10

global competence, lesson examples
  Ancient Number Systems, 42–44
  Earth Sciences, 87–88, 91–93, 96–101
  Examining Laughter in the United States and Afghanistan, 57–59
  Exploring Shelters Across the World, 54–57
  Exposing the Plight of the Colonized, 69–70
  Faxing a Letter to Washington, D.C., 33–34
  Growing Food for the Community, 66–68
  Latin American Literature, 40–42
  Perceptions About HIV/AIDS Across Religious Groups, 44–47
  Promoting the Survival of Andean Musical Heritage, 78–79
  Raising Awareness About Children in Detention Centers, 75–78
  Reflecting on Globalization, 34–36
  Seeking Solutions to a Water Pollution Crisis, 79–82
global competence, teaching for
  assessments, 97–100
  key capacities required, 86–87
  learning goals, requirements of, 92–93
  Pandora questions, 89*f*
  performances of global competence, 94–97
  standards, achieving, 101–102
  topic choice criteria, 90–91
Global Competence Matrix, 143–144
  for the Arts, 144–145
  for English Language Arts, 146–147
  for Mathematics, 147–149
  for Science, 149–150
  for Social Studies, 151–152
  for World Languages, 152–154
global economy, 11, 18–21
globalization
  changes accompanying, 7–10
  class project on, 34–36
  digital connectivity in, 16–18
  labor market, 19–21
Global School Design Blueprint
  assessment, 106–107, 116
  curriculum, 106–107, 111–114
  framework, 105*f*

Global School Design Blueprint
—(*continued*)
  graduate profiles, 109–111
  instruction, 106–107, 114–115
  mission, vision, and culture, 106,
    108–109
  partnerships, 108, 121
  professional development, 107,
    120–121
  school organization and gover-
    nance, 107, 118–120
  student learning outcomes, 106,
    109–111
  world languages, 116–118
graduate profiles, 109–111
graduation requirements, 124–126, 128
Growing Food for the Community
  lesson, 66–68

higher education, role in furthering
  global competence, 140–141

identity, hybrid, 11
Illinois Global Scholar Initiative, 126,
  128
individuals, globally competent
  as agents of change, 27
  characteristics of, 13, 38–39,
    52–53, 64–66, 74–75
  in the digital world, 17–18
  drive toward creating, 123
  examples, 75–82
  in the global economy, 20–21
  global issues, investigating, 13
  relationship building, 13, 26–27
institutional learning domain, 30
instruction, Global School Design
  Blueprint, 106–107, 114–115. *See also*
  global competence, teaching for
intercultural relations learning domain,
  29
interdependence, global, 8–10
interdependence learning domain,
  29–30
International Education Planning
  Rubric: State Strategies to Prepare
  Globally Competent Students, 128
investigating the world dimension of
  global competence
  benefits of, 50–51
  challenges and opportunities, 47–48

investigating the world dimension of
  global competence—(*continued*)
  characteristics of, 38–39
  cognitive developmental progres-
    sions, 49–50f
  lesson examples, 25, 39–47
  overview, 24–25

kindness, 18

Latin American Literature lesson,
  40–42
leadership role in furthering global
  competence, 139
learning, qualities of essential
  depth, 30–32
  engaging the whole person, 28–29
  long-lasting, 32
  relevance, 29–30
learning goals, 92–93, 99
learning outcomes, Global School
  Design Blueprint, 106, 109–111

Malaguzzi, Loris, 4
Mathematics, Global Competence
  Matrix for, 147–149
media literacy, 16–17
migration, global, 10–13
mission, Global School Design Blueprint, 106, 108–109

nationalism, 8

Organisation for Economic Cooperation and Development (OECD)
  framework for global competence,
  9–10, 21–22, 23–24, 24f

Pandora questions, 89f
partnerships, Global School Design
  Blueprint, 108, 121
Perceptions About HIV/AIDS across
  Religious Groups lesson, 44–47
perspectives appreciation dimension
  of global competence
  characteristics of, 52–53
  cognitive developmental progres-
    sions, 61–62f
  environmental stewardship, 16
  global economy, 20
  introduction, 25–26

perspectives appreciation dimension of global competence—(*continued*)
  lesson examples, 26, 33–34, 53–59
  migrant experience, 12–13
  opportunities and challenges, 59–60
policymakers role in furthering global competence, 139–140
poverty as destiny, 124
professional development, 107, 120–121, 129
Programme of International Student Assessment (PISA) global competence cognitive test, 135–137
Promoting the Survival of Andean Musical Heritage lesson, 78–79
public policy, advocating through, 123–133

Raising Awareness About Children in Detention Centers lesson, 75–78
Reflecting on Globalization lesson, 34–36
relationships, building across difference, 13, 26–27
relevance, essential learning for, 29–30

school organization and governance, Global School Design Blueprint, 107, 118–120
schools, globally competent. *See also* Global School Design Blueprint
  advocating for through public policy, 124–133
  educators' capacity, increasing, 128–132
  graduation requirements in, 124–126, 128
  International Education Planning Rubric for, 128
  international examples, 125, 130
  standards redesign in, 124–125
  USDOE Framework for, 126, 127*f*
  worldwide connections, providing opportunities for, 133
Science, Global Competence Matrix for, 149–150
Seeking Solutions to a Water Pollution Crisis lesson, 79–82
Social Studies, Global Competence Matrix for, 151–152

socioeconomic development learning domain, 29–30
standards
  achieving, 101–102
  in essential learning, 32
  redesign in globally competent schools, 124–126, 128
sustainability learning domain, 30

taking action toward collective well-being and sustainable development dimension of global competence
  characteristics of, 74–75
  cognitive developmental progressions, 85*f*
  in the global economy, 20–21
  introduction, 27
  opportunities and challenges, 83–84
teacher preparation programs, 129–130
teachers, role in furthering global competence, 138. *See also* global competence, teaching for
technology access, 16–18
Toronto District School Board case study, 131–132

unemployment, youth, 19
United Nations' Sustainable Development Goals, 9
U.S. Department of Education Framework for Global Competence, 126, 127*f*

vision, Global School Design Blueprint, 106, 108–109

well-being, 19. *See also* taking action toward collective well-being and sustainable development dimension of global competence
workforce requirements, 21st century, 19–21
World Languages, Global Competence Matrix for, 152–154
world languages, Global School Design Blueprint, 116–118
worldviews, understanding others.' *See* perspectives appreciation dimension of global competence

xenophobia, 8